Donald Trump's Teaching:
Deception Is Not Eternal

By: José Armando Pulido Rojas

AKA: Armando X Jop

1

Dignity is the ability to stand tall and strong while facing adversity, while also being able to revere the elders and crawl with the children. Dignity is standing firm in your beliefs without closing your mind to another opinion (Mychal Wynn)

There are two types of pride, the good and the bad. "Good pride" represents our dignity and our self-esteem. "Bad pride" is a mortal sin of superiority that suggests of vanity and arrogance. (John C. Maxwell)

Who and Why is this book written

It has been fascinating to see a US president turn his country and the world upside down although in the past some US presidents have turned down the world, the case of President Donald Trump is different and attractive. Donald Trump was placed in 2016 and since then he has turned the country upside down: He has fought with everyone, has few friends, few love him and no one day has stopped delivering amazing news. So far his job has been to sing the truth about the negative of the system, the falsework of politics, the media, and the international society. Trump considers the system unreliable because he is accused of not paying taxes although all the rich do the same. To fix this, the system hides the theft of taxes by the rich making this an ethical issue if the winning president files his tax return. The purpose of this is to move the common people to pay taxes obediently as the president does. Trump has not obeyed that demand because before being president he was rich and did not pay taxes because the system knows the rich ran many risks creating companies and generating employment. With this refusal Trump defended himself but he also made it clear that people should pay taxes because they should and not because the president also pays.

Like that episode there are many in which Trump shows the hypocrisy and inefficiency of the system, that's why he does not believe or respect the system, that's why everything and almost everyone is against him and that's why Donald Trump's presidency is very interesting because he changed the way of doing politic without diplomacy, without following the rules of the system and singing the truth to everyone through his controversial twitters. Americans accepted Trump because hopelessness had come after hope with Barack Obama faded. Obama, the first African American president, disappointed because he did not cultivate the social balance strongly, the level of the poor did not decrease, but he did increase the bureaucracy and Obama's social environment. This disappointment caused the Americans to seek hope in another candidate who would give them the American dream. Trump made Americans dream of the idea of making America great again, and of a safe border from crime and illegal immigration of Mexicans. Trump won and in his four years in office, he turned the country upside down by ending political diplomacy, attacking the global philosophy, and destroying all the programs that Obama has developed.

Due to the earthquake that Trump generated in politics, in the country, and in the world, it was interesting to record it. I was interested in that political earthquake that broke all the diplomatic rules, leaving the traditional bureaucracy open-mouthed. The astonishment of all was great but the most important thing was that with Trump's rude behavior, the hypocrisy and negligence of those who had always ruled were discovered. Trump's behavior, the failures of the political system, and the harmfulness of traditional politics were revealed with the record of events. Trump's work was recorded in the form of letters, more than a hundred, that I sent him from the beginning of 2019 until after the end of the presidential elections. The letters, sent to the White House server, were intended to guide the president due to his political inexperience, however, they became a testimony of who Trump was as a person, of the shortcomings of the political system of the country and the world, and the permanent neglect of traditional politics. I don't know if they read the letters but they were written with professionalism to show the relevance of the news, the character that Trump applied to it, the reaction of the opposition and the media, and generally gave Trump my best political advice. I knew I could give wise, accurate, and honest advice on politics because I have been educated as a social communicator-journalist, I had completed a master's degree in political science in Seoul, Korea and I had been an active member of the Army.

The result of these reports showed the enthusiastic, narcissistic, rude, angry and unethical character of Trump, and also showed the deficiencies of the political system, the political division due to greed for power; and the real social problems of the country were aired. And from all this it can be inferred that Trump knew very well the deficiencies of the system, that is why he ran the country as he pleased; furthermore, turning the country upside down as Trump did was beneficial because he discovered that politics transformed life into déjà vu where the same social problems are repeated but never resolved. Trump turned everything around to show that the same social problems continue but people do not react and continue to vote for the same politicians, for the same unequal and unfair life, and that the media fill life with fake news

Finally, I began to believe in Trump when I saw that he did not give up on fulfilling his goals by fighting against everyone. Many times his lies disappointed me, but I realized that they were less harmful than those told by traditional politicians who relied on silence and negligence in order to maintain the same social inequality. The conflicting voice of Trump that spoke for those who have no voice in this world, fills me with hope to seek a different way of governing. I transferred this hope to my name to create the nickname that identifies me as a writer. Armando x JOP is the nickname that identifies me as the author of this book but my real name is José Armando Pulido. Probably you have noticed now that nickname and name are related and the nickname suggests some deductions. The nickname and nickname's inferences are this book's essence. Armando x JOP is a similar form of saying in English building for hope. Armando in the Spanish language means 'building' and JOP which is an abbreviation of Jose (JO) Pulido (P) has the same pronunciation as the English word 'hope' (JOP). The red color means the courage that people who build have and the green color signifies hope. In general, the nickname and the book core all is about building for hope or Armando x JOP through our political rights.

INTRODUCTION

In the politics of the US, everything seemed normal, calm, honest, and stable until Donald Trump was appointed as president of the US, a man who had no experience in politics but who knew very well the shortcomings of the system. He started the presidency like an earthquake changing everything by applying rude, impolite, and not very presidential methods. His opponents were surprised at the rude way he handled politics, considering that this would harm the country and the world, so they join forces to attack him without compassion to remove him from the presidency. Despite the attacks and soon completing four years as president, Trump never changed his conflictive character that has turned the country and the world upside down. Trump doesn't seem to care about being liked by anyone but taking advantage of his quarter of an hour by paving the way for his reelection by forming social chaos. But what the president Trump has done so far has it been just for his benefit or really the politics of the country and the world was very bad that it needed a change?

The United State and world politics have been mismanaged and it is the déjà vu that always repeats the same number of social inequality and violence that leaves the common people without hope of living. People need hope to live, they look for a leader to change their lives, they want to put their faith in someone who may bring order, justice, equality, and peace as they did with Jesus Christ more than 2000 years ago, calling him a savior and the king of kings. In 2008, Americans put their faith in Barack Obama; the first African American became the 44th president of the United States and four years later he was reelected. People were eagerly waiting for Obama to bring equality, peace, and enormous development to the world, but it was not like that; instead, he created a huge bureaucracy to protect his personal environment and his party. With Obama the status quo of social differences continued the same, generating discontent in the people of the countryside and small towns that were forgotten. Much of the middle class and young people were also disappointed with Obama because there was not the expected development. In the 2016 election, all those unhappy people looked for another savior and opted for a rich man with no political experience called Donald John Trump.

Observing the debates between Hillary Clinton and Donald Trump that gave him victory in 2016, it was appreciated that Donald Trump wanted to win the presidency at any cost regardless of respect and ethics rules. Trump attacked the candidate Hillary Clinton rudely threatening to put her in jail when he became president for endangering the security of the country by sending emails without due protection as Secretary of State. Such rude debates had never been seen in the country and this could have motivated those weak in spirit. Trump also made promises that he knew he could not fulfill as it was to build the border wall with Mexico of more than 3000 kilometers and that Mexico will pay for the construction. This promise coming from a rich man also motivated many people to vote for him because the border would be a reality that would improve the security of the country. Thus knowing of his defects and that it had also been aired in the media that Trump was a womanizer, that he cheated with taxes, that he was not loyal to his friends, the Americans put Trump to lead the White House.

But were people so desperate that they decided to hand over the power of the most powerful country to a man with no political experience and with so many imperfections? When Barack Obama ended the presidency in 2017 the country functioned normally with a stable economy; in that state, another traditional politician could have been the president and the country would have avoided the experience of Donald Trump. However, Obama's departure left the taste of disenchantment because social equality did not occur, minorities made little progress, and Obama was seen as one of the bureaucratic politicians. At that time the Democratic Party had lost power and the Republicans had the Senate and governed more states than the Democrats. The hope that was had for a black president was vanished and now it seemed that the déjà vu of a lifetime would follow. Nothing seemed to motivate the disappointing social sectors until they felt the bravery of Donald Trump and heard his infinite promises.

Trump came with the desire to change everything Barack Obama has done and knew how to do it because he knew the power of the executive body. Trump started changing everything but not only because he hated Obama but because it was part of his advertising character and it was also part of a political strategy. The strategy of changing everything is used in the construction business that parties and business compromise does not break down because there is a project to accomplish. As an expert in the construction business, Trump knows that the business is tied up from the signing of the contract and the demolition. From the beginning Trump used this strategy because he planned his government to two terms: in the first period, there would be important work unfinished and the voters would reelect him to complete the work in the second period. There are really important jobs to be completed now: a healthy immigration law, the wall on the border with Mexico, a health plan for all, employing all Americans, improving the economy, reducing the power of China, limit the spread of communism and terrorism and achieve peace in the Middle East by supporting Israel and finish the movie with North Korea. Trump has bet on this strategy of forcing continuity due to the many works he has in development, and also because generating news is part of Trump's character to attract attention.

Trump sought the presidency not because he knew how to run the country or wanted to do it well but because it was the position where he could feed the ego, where everyone would listen to him and appreciate him. Trump had reached the dream position from where he could best practice his narcissistic character. Losing reelection will be frustrating because Trump will lose the microphone and the scenarios that make him happy by showing people his power and courage. Trump is narcissistic and needs to be nurturing ideas of greatness. Acquaintances of Trump say that no one enjoys a presidential campaign, speaking in public and touring the country more than Donald Trump. Trump may not know what he is talking about in speeches, but he is happy to be applauded and recognized by the public. With the election only a few days away, Trump knows he has made many mistakes managing the country which is why he now relies on the Machiavellian part of his character attacking with any means, especially by sending lies, accusations, and offensive messages by Twitter.

This book is not about Trump's character but about his work in the last two years of administration which can reveal his character, his work philosophy, let see if he was qualified to be president if the Americans were right when naming him and deserve to be reelected or they made a grave mistake electing him. Americans can infer all that through reading this writing that has the form of letters that I sent to the president because like many Americans I felt disappointed with Obama and I decided to put my faith in Trump too, giving him my political advice. I am not American I am from Colombia but everywhere people are looking for a leader who can end the déjà vu in politics that always repeats the social inequality, the same episodes of injustice, violence, and corruption. Trump was another option, different, without political experience but rich and with experience in business that could help to end corruption, improve the economy, and so give social equality.

There are almost one hundred letters sent to the White House server from January 2019 until just before the 2020 election. This period was chosen because it was unprecedented in registering a dirty war between parties as a result of having a singular president who has no experience in politics, want to be against the system, and always want to win using dirty methods; on the other side, the opposition party wants to remove him from office using any means. On the side of Trump, there are significant moments that show his character and political procedures to solve problems: although Trump had said that Mexico would pay for the border wall since he did not comply, Trump collected resources by ignoring the system and discrediting the past administration. This episode showed his unwavering passion to win at any cost. He made the longest government shutdown in the history of the country to pressure the Senate for resources. In the end, he got something but not enough, then Trump declares a national emergency to get resources from the pentagon and other sources without touching the Senate. Here he makes it clear that he did not believe or respect the system; he believes the system works leisurely and he needed money fast to build the wall. Meanwhile, Trump blamed the Obama administration for the soft immigration policy that filled the country with crime and violence, that's why to protect the country, Trump needed to build the border with Mexico.

On the Democratic side, since Trump started his administration democrats made a vulgar war to try to remove Trump from office. It was two years of investigation looking at Trump's connections with Russia to win the presidency in 2016. The counselor, Mr. Robert Mueller, couldn't find conclusive evidence and in the end, Mueller released a document where he unconfined Trump from any charge. It was a fiasco for democrats because they expected positive charges to prosecute Trump, and it was worse after the attorney general, Mr. William Barr, through an informs confirmed the absolution. But Democrats didn't stop their tyranny against Trump and the House Judiciary Committee started a parallel investigation looking for pieces of evidence that Trump colluded with Russia to win the election. This investigation didn't work out but the good luck looked for democrats when a whistleblower appeared affirming that the president had pressed the Ukraine president to investigate the former vice president and Democratic candidate Joe Biden. Democrats considered it was a crime of abuse of power made by the president and it was the perfect chance to impeach him.

Nothing of these grave charges seems to worry Trump conversely, Trump seems to be enjoying the situation generating all kinds of news every day by any means, sending aggressive twitters or by giving polemic informs to the media. It seems Trump wasn't interested in getting good poll numbers, he was just interested in to show the infinite power he had. At the same time, Trump continued working as nothing was happening but always creating polemics. For example, Trump visited the North Korean leader Kim Jong Un in the North Korea border but it seemed more a show to show himself doing something that previous administrations have not done, but this meeting wasn't really for looking North Korea denuclearization or unite the two Koreas. The same happened with other Trump's decisions that seemed part of a show where he wants to show his power but it seems he didn't know why he was making those decisions. That was the case of canceling the denuclearization agreement with Iran, the commercial agreement with Cuba that both were made by the former president Barack Obama, and also the case of starting a commercial war with China that seems to have no end.

Those were grave problems for the country and President Trump knows about but unfortunately, he doesn't have a serious plan to solve this instead he is using those matters to get acceptance. In the case of Iran, this country continues supporting terrorist groups; in Cuba, freedoms are restricted, and China has been getting benefits from the US for more than thirty years and it has used those benefits to extent communism around the world and become a powerful country. Many Americans agreed with Trump about that and many other problems but they want also to see a soon solution. Trump has also been the first president who has aired the media problem that exhibits fake news; no previous presidents did that revelation before although they knew about the media's fake news and some presidents supported the fake news for their own benefit. That's why for ventilating problems that politicians have been hidden for a long time many Americans support Trump and like his courage.

There are some problems more than others that interest Trump and he openly supports or rejects them without fear of criticism. He has rejected openly global plans to protect climate change, receiving anger notes from many world leaders. Trump considers the climate change problem is not of the magnitude that is painted and the world organisms in charge of protecting the environment are bureaucrats earning money for themselves but aren't changing anything. If this rejection has shocked, Trump's rejection of globalization and multilateralism has angered more. Trump has been faithful to his national government program that looks first to the US than other countries and international organisms. Trump has not had a good relationship with G-20 and G-7 groups, and neither the European Union and lately with the OMS because he probably thinks globalization is dividing the US making lose its economic power while China and other countries are taking advantage. That's why since the beginning of Trump's administration, he has been focused on making America great again which means to protect the US border to make safer the country; immigrants will be accepted by merits, and the country economy will be focused on supporting the Americans first.

In the same way, as Trump is interested in his country Trump is also interested in the peace of the Middle East. The Middle East problem should ashamed previous administrations because they have just used this matter as a political campaign but they haven't solved there anything. To try to solve this problem, Trump has been more precise but without abandoning the spectacle. In general, Trump wants Israel to be the leader of the region by being the capital center of the region and by gaining many allies from Arab countries. So Israel and its allies can control the routes used by Iran to spread terrorism, weakening Iran, and can also lead a plan to achieve peace with Palestine. All that, Trump has been achieved with spectacular actions that let them see his interest in calling public attention and for showing his resolution. Trump did something that called the attention of the world and caused anger to Palestinians after he located the American embassy in Jerusalem. With this action Trump was saying to Israel: from now you are the leader of the region. Also, Trump made a detailed military action against Iran to teach Iran that it is better to negotiate. Using drones, the US forces killed Qasem Soleimani, the most important general of Iran who used to make plans to kill American soldiers in Iraq. Finally, Trump has achieved a reconciliation with Arab countries and Israel, creating an Israel force of allies to weaken Iran.

When everything seemed to be going well for Trump because the economy was at its best, growing and with low unemployment; also the Senate had voted in favor of Trump to close the impeachment case, the virus Covid 19 unfortunately consumed the world becoming a pandemic. As Trump has handled the pandemic so far, many people have criticized him but many too have supported him, and this problem has revealed Trump's character clearly. Before the pandemic, Trump thought he had everything ready to win the reelection because the economy was fine, but with the pandemic, the economy went to the ground and it seems the reelection too. Then Trump started looking for perpetrators and found that the virus had originated in China and the OMS has not acted soon. Trump couldn't be quiet and denounced that China and the OMS were responsible for the pandemic. Trump remained faithful to his plan to grow the economy without frightening people about the virus, so he was not demanding preventive measures such as the use of masks and prudent physical distance. So far the US is the country in the world with more dead and infected but does not seem to worry about Trump. Trump seems to be enjoying the pandemic being news every day on the number of deaths, on his idea of not believing in the pandemic, and on attacking China and the OMS.

Trump as many people may think that the pandemic could be a plot to remove Trump from power organized by China and the OMS. That could be a conspiracy theory but it has a lot of truth. The pandemic was announced by the OMS because the OMS is a world health organization and it, in a few seconds, closed the world. The OMS took that decision after China warned about the presence of the Covid 19 and its danger. But this danger appears precisely in the year of elections and when the relationship with China was at its worst. Trump announced that the OMS worked in complicity with China to remove him from power, and Trump decided not to give the OMS more resources. Trump also explained the pandemic was a plot to remove him from power because the OMS had not declared the pandemic in the past for many other diseases. However, no one including his opponents expected Trump reacted to the pandemic as he did without fear, accepting its costs, being irresponsible but enjoying being different taking risks, and being hated by many and appreciated by many too.

Donald Trump may lose the reelection but despite that and Trump's many imperfections he has achieved many positive things during this first period, and in the last two months of the campaign, he has shown he is tireless and has energy for four more years. Trump's imperfections have helped him to put up with attacks from everywhere and have also given vitality to do all the things he has done every day for four years. Trump is a 74 years man and during the four years as president has worked more than twelve hours every day and it is for Trump's personality of being always a winner, never a loser, nurturing his ego and self-admiration. Those are Trump's motors of energy that make him a sick liar but also achieve everything that is proposed. Without those motors of vitality, Trump would not have survived the four years of government because he was alone against the world. Trump endured the fiercest media attacked every day during four years; also endured a two-year investigation and won the impeachment process that was intended to remove him from office. Trump gave positive for Covid 19 creating great controversy but he continues working as nothing had happened, and also achieved the great triumph of appointing judge Amy Coney Barrett to the Supreme Court, giving confidence to the Republican Party and providing a conservative line to the country.

If Trump is or not reelected his presidency needs to be considered the most important in US history. Trump changed the way of working and understanding politics. He finished the diplomacy singing trues openly to everyone, so Americans could understand now how they have been cheated lifetime by traditional politicians, how globalization and world organisms are other deceptions, how the left is growing affecting freedom and world security, and how the media affects people presenting fake news. Trump can be considered the bigger liar in US history but he used lies to protect himself from traditional politicians who wanted to destroy him, but he let see that lies from traditional politicians have been more harmful because they do not fulfill anything and have delayed the country especially increasing social inequality. One example of fraud is the former vice president Joe Biden who has been in politics for more than forty years and he hasn't done anything significant and so traditional politicians has always acted. Instead, Trump has managed to revive political life saying that it is important to work for America and Americans and so has worked tirelessly these four years. Trump can have many defects but he is a man of action who works hard to produce positive results. I think opting for Biden is to continue with the more dangerous deceiver but electing Trump means getting progress, courage, and above all entertainment every day. But if Biden wins, he will have the lesson of Trump who showed the deficiencies of the system so that Biden can correct that and offer development for the country and justice, respect, and equality to Americans.

Letters

YOU MUST TEACH THAT YOU ARE IN CHARGE

29 January 2019

Mr. President, you must be courteous to the people and arrogant to the Democrats and the media because the people are necessary while the media and the Democrats are not necessary because they deceive the people. These days you have experienced the discourtesy of Nancy Pelosi, the spokesperson for the House of Representatives, who did not announce the invitation to give the annual State of the Union speech. You acted well ignoring her rudeness because this is an acquired right as president. Pelosi believes that you do not deserve to enter the House of Representatives or give that speech, but she is wrong because it was the Americans who gave you that right. Nancy Pelosi finally invites you to give the State of the Union speech, and the media shows you as a loser. Pelosi may be seen as the American Thatcher, but she is far away of look like Ms. Thatcher. Americans may consider that Pelosi has more power than the President has because she decided when you can give the Union Speech. You may remove that misconception by explaining there what things are wrong in the country to make America great again and the things you need to accomplish. You have to emphasize how you want to make America great again and you won't accept negations. To elaborate the speech, you need to remember what happened during the shutdown when Democrats went on vacation while you were working, demonstrating Democrats just care about themselves.

NATIONAL EMERGENCY TO SAVE THE WALL

01 February 1, 2019

Mr. President, the past administrations were more concerned with cultivating their power than with the internal security of the country, that is why the border is a heap of garbage and junk that identifies the political class that governed. If the United States were an insignificant country, security would not be important, it would not be the target of crime and global enemies. But the United States is a power envied and desired by many. That is why security is one of the priorities of your government. You are now worried about getting money to build the border wall with Mexico. Your son and many Americans agree to declare a national emergency to get resources from other sources. Mr. President does not worry about external comments, you are doing the right action to improve the country. Most of the US security problems come from the southern border and those might increase if the government doesn't take radical actions now. A well-constructed wall might end illegal immigration and crimes that come from Mexico. It has been proved that Democrats don't want to support the idea of building the wall; so it is wise to look for other ways to fund the wall. If you want Americans to see you as a leader who may accomplish goals, the border wall has to start to be built this year. You can make plans faster if you declare the national emergency and it will be less complicated because you don't need Congress's approval, neither

Democrats' support. There are enough resources stored for emergencies that will not be used; you could use that money because the law allows you when there is a crisis of security Mr. President goes ahead with your plan and trust in your intuition.

TAKE CARE YOUR BACK

February 12, 2019

Mr. President, distrust, being a vigilant maniac, and being foresighted are the actions that I recommend you adopt to improve your security and that of the country. You have already realized that you have many enemies, and the best thing to do is to take good care of your back. The 2020 presidential campaign has already started and you have to look carefully because there are around many enemies who try to destroy you. Firstly, the enemy has infiltrated your house; last week they filtered your personal schedule. Mr. President, I personally don't like Mick Mulvaney, the chief of staff, try to observe him carefully; Democrats and fake news are going to do anything to stop the presidential reelection; try always to be a step ahead accomplishing what you had promised to people and denouncing Democrats' illegal actions. The first step to win is to take care of your back carefully, and the second is to show Americans that you can accomplish what you promised. The US is a very rich country but it is an unsafe one because of illegal immigration. It is not fair for people to live with fear in a rich country. People will be grateful to you if you may build the southern border wall where insecurity goes into the US. Mr. President, you have the legal tools to do it, please use them effectively.

KEEP IN GOOD SHAPE

February 16, 2019

Mr. President, I believe that the human being is defined by the things he eats and how he eats them; eating fast, cheap, and easy is not good. Also being very fat is not good for health, personal comfort, or aesthetics. Now that there are many things to do after declaring the national emergency, you need to be in good shape. Because of your fast food taste, I know you have ordered this meal for some of your White House guests. Also, I knew you have put on extra pounds over the past year, but it is better to be thin because bones are not strong enough to support 120 kilograms. If you are overweight, you become tired faster and sicknesses come easily too. Please try to follow an exercise routine and also a plan for eating better.

I know you like fast food and fillet of steak well done with fry potatoes; it is delicious food. There is not any reason to stop eating that delicious food, but if you want to reduce weight it has to be eating in smalls amounts every three hours. In that way, you may achieve two goals one is you may continue enjoying the food, and two, you may train the brain to eat moderately. About exercising you can ask the doctor about the best one to reduce weight. Mr. President, please take care of yourself because there are too many things to work on.

CHANGE PAST MISTAKES

February 23, 2019

Mr. President, what the traditional political class has done so far in the United States is a dictatorship; therefore, change and revolution become a right. Change is achieved by applying a new model, and the nationalist model that you propose can end social injustice. Hopeless people hope to see their country grow inward to live properly and in peace. You also don't seem concerned about having any political experience, but this weakness is meant to be used as a political weapon to attack you. Before being president many people said you cannot be one because don't have the experience, but experience has been used by politicians to evade responsibilities. Now thank to you, people have been able to realize what things are wrong in politics. Mr. President, you have a great chance of changing two areas which are affecting the country seriously. One is the Democratic Party that has not done anything for the country; these party members have gotten benefits just for themselves. That is why the US looks like an undeveloped country having an old and bad infrastructure. The other serious problem is the media. They always spread fake news; the media don't do any good job. People realized how badly the media work during the last shutdown. Journalists were always attacking the shutdown without showing evidence about anything. Journalists are not doing their job correctly, they are just speculating and it is very dangerous. Mr. President, the future of the country is in your hands and to achieve this experience in politics is not the most important thing; I think, the most important thing is to give dignity to the people by making the country powerful again following a nationalist line.

BE ONE STEP AHEAD

February 24, 2019

Mr. President, even if you think to improve the security of the country, you should sleep with only one eye because the enemy is close to you. I believe something really bad is being planned to hurt you. It is not any doubt the evil plan comes from the Democratic Party. During the eight years of Obama's administration, the party got enough power and can do anything to abolish you. So please be careful and try always to be one step ahead. Mr. President, you can see by yourself the signs and figure out what the plan is about. One mark is that Mr. Muller, the special counsel, won't give his report until next week because he may be waiting for more information from Michael Cohen, your former attorney, and from the Northern District of New York that is checking your finances. Muller really wants to have a great victory fighting your case, he wants to be remembered as a hero. He doesn't want to give up seeing you in prison. I think you have to attack, too. No one before has investigated Democrat presidents as you have been investigated. However, you may order to investigate former President Obama and his vice president Biden. They all were negligent in doing the work suitably that is why the country is backward and insecure. Mr. President tries to be always a step ahead.

KIM JONG- UN APPRECIATE YOU

March 2, 2019

Mr. President, it is difficult to admire the president of North Korea, but the unknown does produce admiration; I believe it is the moment to know the truth of this country and its dictator to make a good negotiation. As a good businessman, you know that you have to create customer trust, and you have applied the same with the Korean leader. Despite some media bad comments about the summit with Mr. Kim Jong- un, North Korea President, I believe it was successful. As you said it is walking to also I can say, it is giving steps toward you want. This kind of negotiation is like conquering a girl's heart: first, she needs to feel confident, and then she will start to show signs. I believe, Mr. Kim will soon start to give answers.

Everyone even the media needs to understand that it is hard to gain Kim's trust because he is a communist person and distrusts capitalism. However, Mr. President, you obtained Kim's trust in the two summits letting him talk and be close to you. You have not criticized anything of Kim and he has learned that it is possible to negotiate with people who have different ideologies. Mr. Kim may be thinking now you are an easy-going person who can negotiate and believes he has the right channel to negotiate. Mr. President, as you use to say you made a good job, you also did it in Hanoi.

THE MEDIA IS DANGEROUS

March 3, 2019

Mr. President, journalism consists of people who cannot write, who have no culture or ethics to cultivate the global ignorance of the people. I believe you are the first president who tells the truth to the media that they are irresponsible, liars, and are destroying the country; so there is an urgent necessity of modifying the media performance. The media is doing what they want irresponsibly, they are not doing responsibly what the country needs. The whole media action is directed toward defending who they like or destroying who they hate. The media has to be impartial and dedicated to providing real news that may guide people to make decisions correctly. Unfortunately, journalists act in the opposite direction that could be proven by observing news about your trip to Hanoi.

The media has ignored the North Korea summit and has tried to destroy you while you were absent from the country. The media focused on your former attorney, Michael Cohen, waiting he could say something that may incriminate you. As Cohen repeated the same words that he had said much time before, those words did not clarify anything, just concluded the same: there is no collusion. Disappointed, journalists were looking to discredit you more. Then the media attacked the summit in Hanoi. Irresponsibly without analysis and facts, they titled the summit was a fiasco; Trump got nothing in Hanoi; the summit was a failure. Mr. President, Hanoi's episode can confirm that the media is managed by dishonest and irresponsible people. While you were in Hanoi, YouTube and CNN exhibits all your family in jail wearing orange dresses; attacking the president irresponsibly and suggesting jail you without a legal process, that is not the media role. Please, try to change the media's bad behavior and lack of ethics for the good of the country.

RHETORIC AND FACTS ARE YOUR TOOLS

March 7, 2019

Mr. President, politicians have made the people fall in love with words but have disappointed by the lack of facts; I think that the mixture between words and real facts makes people fall in love; but if there are only facts, words are unnecessary. This moment is very difficult politically; therefore you must use an effective strategy to defend yourself. The media and the Democratic Party want to disclose every aspect of your business and private life. They really want to bury you politically. You always wanted to be a politician, and now that you are in may understand how politics is dirty and difficult to handle. You may feel tired, stress, and sad now, but you cannot give up. You just need to rethink how the future can be managed better.

My advice today is that you have to mix rhetoric and facts. So far you have used rhetoric and it has worked out, but at this moment the things are different because you are trapped in the middle of the game and cannot dessert. They want to destroy you with facts because it is easy to find mistakes about you. As you have abilities in rhetoric, try now to shape credible facts. You need credible facts to defend yourself; the facts you need are about people who try to destroy you as journalists, lawmakers, counsels, lawyers. Also, try to have credible documents about your business because the enemy wants to attack that front.

The other important thing is to make your word a fact. It means you promised people to build the northern border wall, and you have to do that. If you build the wall, the American people will trust you and vote for you in the 2020 election. Mr. President, I could see a factual action today showing how the enemy can be attacked effectively. CNN will be indicted for covering news wrongly and will be charged with 250 million dollars. I believe attacking with facts is the best way to defend yourself.

FAKE NEWS IS THE ENEMY OF THE PEOPLE

March 20, 2019

Mr. President, the term fake news from the media arrived with your administration and it seems that the term removed a blindfold from the people of the world. Fake news is trying to make you feel bad and to draw a bad image of you. Any wrong thing that happens around the world, fake news makes you responsible for. Fake news always titles badly against you. They are now saying you are crazy because tweeted many lies, affirming you're a maniac liar. No one had attacked other presidents before as fake news is doing to you now. I understand it makes you feel bad but they just want you to give up.

Million Americans trust you, but fake news tries to hide your realizations. People follow your idea about making America great again. Those Americans don't trust the traditional politic because it hasn't done anything to make America great before. Mr. President, every traditional politician is against you, but try to look at that opposition as a positive one. It is because when you have acted avoiding lobbyists, you have allowed discovering how much corrupt the traditional politic is. Mr. President, you have to be proud of yourself; it just remembers how much corruption was exposed during the last shutdown when Democrats and some Republicans evaded responsibilities and it was shown that they have made an elite who manage the resources as they want.

Also during the shutdown, Americans realized how corrupt the media is. They don't display sources nor data they just giving wrong opinions. The media is going to destroy the world if someone doesn't stop the media's irresponsible work. However, you have given the first step showing that the media is really fake news media. Mr. President, don't give up on your ideas nor the presidency; try to find good advisers who work looking at real data, display always real data, and also be one step ahead attacking your enemies with real data.

THE MEDIA WITHOUT ETHICS

April 5, 2019

Mr. President, the Colombian writer Gabriel Garcia Marquez affirmed that the journalist must have a great cultural base, a lot of practice but above all ethics; of all that there is only practice lacking in culture and ethics. Ethics is that human behavior that indicates what is right or wrong, good and bad; however, the media forgot it. The US has had lately two important episodes that have shown how badly the media work. The first one was the shutdown early this year ordered by your administration seeking to fund the southern wall. The other ended last week with general attorney William Barr's report when absolved you of conspiracy after two years of the investigation conducted by the special counsel Robert Muller. In both episodes, the media showed partiality in defending its own ideas, and Democratic Party but attacking you without proved sources and declaring personal opinions.

Now that the shutdown has finished and Muller's report has been submitted, the media has lost its credibility totally. You survived the obstinate attack with 40 percent of popularity. No president would have survived that hard media assault. After ending the shutdown, you continued the plan of funding the wall by seeing other ways; and after Muller's report remarked that you were innocent, those facts showed that the media has published fake news for two years. I think it is a perfect moment to modify the media's role in society. The media has to be managed by responsible people who provide correct information. And I think you are the right person to change it because has power and began early to denounce the fake news.

THE INVESTIGATION IS OVER, THAT'S THE LAW

May 5, 2019

Mr. President, Democrats are bad losers, they do not accept their crimes but want to endorse them on others. House of Representatives doesn't want to accept as valid the investigation's result and try to open a new investigation citing to declare witnesses and the attorney general. You were declared innocent and lawmakers want to investigate you again. How you should act to avoid being impeached? You don't need to play the game Democrats want to play. Nixon was impeached because he gave to the opposition what they need; you don't have to that. Democrats want to continue the investigation because they want to impeach you before the 2020 election. That's not an investigation that's a dirty political maneuver. Mr. President has to remain firm saying the investigation is over and doesn't accept another investigation. You must also block from giving additional information and block citation to witnesses to testify again. You could also make a contra attack that orders the attorney general to investigate those who investigate you. There are pieces of evidence showing that the investigation started because Democrats spied your campaign in 2016. Spying a party during a campaign is a crime. Mr. President has to attack the opposition but also the press because it has been an accomplice of the crime committed by Democrats

WHOEVER, RESPECT THE PRESIDENT

May 25, 2019

Mr. President, many do not understand that you are now the authority chosen by the people and must be respected. The House of Representatives led by its speaker Nancy Pelosi has increased its attacks against you subpoenaing staff who already declared for two years during special counsel investigation to whom has also subpoenaed as well as the attorney general, William Barr. This week, Democrats seem to be decided to start an impeachment inquiry to you. This situation appears to be very hard but if you observe the things you can find a clever solution. The solution isn't complicated, you have to force Democrats to learn to respect and protect the presidency, whoever the president is.

Democrats started an expensive investigation for two years that concluded the president didn't collude against the US. This decision was not accepted by Democrats and started a new investigation subpoenaing who already was investigated. Now when the 2020 election is around the corner, Democrats want to block you to be reelected by accusing. At this moment the solution is to reeducate the Democrats by teaching them to accept the defeats, support the presidency and legislate for the country.

Mr. President, you also have to address to Americans to explain to them where all this problem comes from in order it doesn't repeat and everyone helps to make America great again. Current US's Problems basically come from a big bureaucracy created by past administrations: the bureaucracy administrated for its own benefit, forgetting the country's progress. The country is behind in tech, infrastructure, health benefits, education, and immigration rules. This presidency has faced all those problems with courage while at the same time, the bureaucracy tries to destroy you by impeaching, stopping the country's progress, and getting again the power to rule in its own favor.

DEMOCRATS WANT TO PUT YOU IN JAIL

June 6, 2019

Mr. President, I don't think you would consider going to jail but the Democrats do want to put you there. The conflictive environment is growing in the House of Democrats as lawmakers try to force the impeachment inquiry process against you. Democrats' persistent idea about impeachment has created a division of the caucus, cannot draw other objectives, has lost its legislative role and Americans now don't understand what the House is for. You should use the wrong direction the House is having currently to ask Democrats to stop the hate and begin to work for the country.

To get reconciliation, House Speaker Nancy Pelosi, who seems to hate you enormously, could be the best way because surprisingly she thinks and acts more rationally than the other lawmakers. Try to follow her ideas that although she wants to put you in jail she wants to do that by a constitutional form letting Americans decide in the 2020 presidential election. So at this moment, she is opposed to prosecuting you, something that some Democrats disagree with radically.

Pelosi's plan to place you in jail means to collect reliable evidence that may indict you, defame you, confirming you have violated the constitution and laws, and so make you arrive weak into the next election. If you lose reelection, Pelosi understands you have lost all the political power and at that point, she will indict you and all the system goes against you. To evade Pelosi's plan, you have to act in Pelosi's opposite direction: do not deliver any evidence, discredit the House of Democrats saying they are doing nothing for the country but just censuring the president.

ONLY PEOPLE SUFFER FROM BAD GOVERNMENTS

June 8, 2019

Mr. President, everyone knows that you hate communism, and rightly so because the rulers there lack thoughts and feelings. You made a deal with Mexico to stop the arrival of illegal immigrants from Mexico and Central America. Mexico's president chose between two options and the best was to negotiate with the US rationally. Manuel Lopez Obrador, Mexico's president, instead of accepting the rise in tariffs suggested by the US if Mexico did not stop the illegal immigration, opted for securing more the country borders. With this decision, Obrador avoided increasing the price of goods caused by rising tariffs that were going to affect Mexicans wages.

This agreement is important because Mexico's president is showing responsibility to govern. Some countries don't care about the US's economic sanctions and it is because they really don't care about people's economy and life. There are many examples of countries that don't care about people's welfare: China, Venezuela, Cuba, Guatemala, Nicaragua, Haiti, Honduras, and others. Those countries don't rule for the people, they rule for a corrupt system and politicians' benefit. The lack of interest in people is a serious problem because this is increasing the number of poor people who cannot wait to starve and opt to immigrate to another country or become criminals.

Venezuela is the most recent example of arousing immigration through increasing poverty. Venezuela's government was just interested in getting the power and putting the country in the hands of the communists. Communists got the country with its political and military power and now it is defending its new property with determination. Communists just cared about Venezuela's land which is a strategic area; so it erased any democratic process and named a perpetual president. Venezuela's president, Nicolas Maduro, is now a dictator who created fear, stimulated poverty and immigration because he is just interested in owning the land with unthinking and subordinated people.

Mr. President, those countries could have made a deal as that you signed with the Mexican president to protect people's wages and life but they didn't. I think it is time to change the variable of applying economic sanctions to the whole country and instead look at a form to sanction individual countries' presidents. Countries' presidents are really responsible for increasing poverty, lack of working opportunities, for weakening borders as well as immigration rules. Countries' people don't have to suffer the effects of the economic sanctions, people are not responsible for the president's corruption, and really who must suffer any sanction has to be the president for not doing his work accurately.

BALANCE BETWEEN ECONOMY AND ENVIRONMENT

June 9, 2019

About the phenomenon of climate change, Mr. President, this became a bureaucratic matter that cares more about money than the environment. Everybody around the world became shocked because after you took the presidency you gave up continuing with the Paris climate agreement. However, since you took this decision there have not been major protests around the world and it is because there is no consensus on the reality of climate change. Some may agree with your point of view and another with scientists' results. The division that exists on this subject is due mainly to the effects of the economy on the environment, but it is important not to ignore this subject, trying to solve it without affecting the economy.

Mr. President, you have realized the Paris climate agreement put limits that affect the economic development of the US. The limits are about using greenhouse gases which the US mainly uses to develop its economy. You have considered that it is important to continue using those fuels at their maximum level to ensure the economy. You have given two reasons to defend your view: One reason is that the greenhouse effect is a natural effect that the earth has to suffer necessarily. The other reason is that the global warming phenomenon became a political matter that populists, socialists, and communists want to get political profits.

However, it is necessary to try also to understand the reasons provided by scientists to avoid future disasters or to find solutions that agree well environment and economy. Scientists have affirmed that global warming has increased because greenhouse gases level has grown, and as they are heavy, they remain on earth causing warming. Currently, there is nothing that can absorb or expel the heavy gases because tree deforestation isn't controlled and there are not enough trees that may reduce the heat. Scientists have mentioned some consequences such as the rise in sea level, the salinity of the sea has increased, the harvests have diminished and the heat causes more deaths.

This topic became important this week because the press said you ordered not to release a scientific document that describes the earth warming problem. I understand you don't want to worry about Americans and want to show great economic results but try to accomplish your goal as you want to look at a balance between progress and the environment. To achieve the atmosphere balance you can recommend ideas for its protection, and I believe everyone will support you because you are the leader of the world currently. You can suggest something that doesn't affect your goal as to ask countries to grow a certain number of trees per year, to give more education about environmental protection and norms about human behavior. Doing that, everyone may appreciate your interest in preserving the planet.

WATERGATE IS NOT YOUR CASE

June 12, 2019

Mr. President, this time is different from that of Nixon, now there is no loyalty in politics, you must defend yourself only with passion. John Dean's comments, the former counsel of President Richard Nixon, need to be analyzed with pincers. With this specific guest in the House of Representatives, Democrats are showing they are not in rush to impeach you instead they want to do the right actions to impeach you effectively. Democrats believe the right action to follow is to light Americans about the need to impeach you. So illustrating Americans over that you really obstructed justice and deserve to be impeached was the main reason the House invited John Dean.

The parallel done between Watergate and Mr. Muller's report can work out and in the end, Congress and Americans could end up supporting this idea and maybe Don McGahn, your former counsel, also end betraying you as John Dean did with President Richard Nixon in 1973. This move made by Democrats has to be studied carefully because the pieces of the parallel are married well and I believe the House is going to continue acting in the same way because they want to weaken and trial you.

Mr. President, I believe you should act in two ways to protect yourself. One, If John Dean said that like in Watergate there was a clear map and in the present investigation about Russia there is also a clear map on Muller's report; so Dean may think the key pieces of the map have to be on your hand. Mr. President, you have to protect data that may affect you and the country's security, protecting data is an executive privilege. Second, if Democrats want to discredit the executive, you have to act in the same way saying John Dean is an opportunist person who won reputation after he was involved in the Watergate betraying president Nixon and currently, Dean wants to wash away his guilt affirming that all presidents after Nixon have acted worse than Watergate. Mr. President, it is clear John Dean has no principles.

WORDS ARE WEAPONS

June 14, 2019

Mr. President, you are a very particular president because you do not measure your words that is why you are not a politician. After reading your comment about accepting dirt information from foreign countries which have been criticized by both parties even by closer allies of you, I want to suggest that it is important to take care of what you say to unite more than divide your confederates. Words are more dangerous than weapons; you must know perfectly that especially in politics where any word is taken for granted. My suggestion is to apply some rules to speak well before speaking: don't add unnecessary comments, don't say everyone is acting wrong because no one wants to hear that, your words have always to support the whole establishment and finally, words are for describing your achievements widely and for discrediting your opponents.

The 2020 election will be a hard contest and from now you need to add instead of subtracting votes. The direct form you pronounce your ideas is a good way to add votes, but the episode about taking dirt information from foreign countries could subtract support. You could have omitted the generalizations that everyone uses dirt information from foreign countries. That affirmation includes Democrats and Republicans and no one wants to be pointed and less in something hard to prove. At this moment, some will be against you but later when it is known that you have confirmed by words that you have done it, everyone could attack you. Mr. President that statement was a risk and I think was unnecessary.

Another unnecessary comment was to say that you would not comment with the FBI about the dirt information. Mr. President, you know everyone defends and supports the establishment, so your statement could make everyone goes against you and instead defend the FBI. Your affirmation became more outrageous after you said the FBI cannot investigate this matter because not have enough personnel and resources. At this point, you were discrediting the FBI but also were discrediting yourself because you have to make the FBI strong.

However, this matter can also be clarified by words. I think I understand when you said there is no problem with listening to someone who has information. There is a big difference between hearing from a person who comes to you and sending someone to spy or ask for information. The first is an unexpected action and the latter is consciously planned, that is why this is criminal. Democrats should understand well the difference between receiving information and spying; spying your campaign was what Democrats did during the 2016 election.

I may also understand when you said you will put the foreign information in the hands of the FBI if you believe there is something wrong. I assume you mean if the information is fraudulent and its only purpose is damaging the opponent, then you put it in the hands of the FBI. Democrats know a lot about disclosing false information to damage the opponent because they did it affirming you conspired with Russia during the 2016 election.

SARAH SANDER WAS A WARRIOR

June 15, 2019

Mr. President, you know the power of the media, but not because of that power you have been afraid of them. Now that Sarah Sanders, the White House press secretary, leaves this work it is necessary to realize that Sarah's role as press secretary was very hard because it was like stopping a mighty river and then change its course. The mighty river is the bourgeois press built during Obama's administration. The press was a well-selected elite who enjoy the whole White House honey and did all that they wished. Obama always praised the press in the annual dinner meeting of the press, there, he performed his jokes demonstrating close partnership and declared his gratitude. Basically, this relationship made a servile press who did very little opposition to Obama.

This press-elite remained for eight years with Obama and wanted to continue with Hillary Clinton. The press showed Hillary its support openly during the 2016 campaign attacking you because were the stronger opponent. The media felt frustrated after you won the presidency and they began the most destructive attack against you, becoming it harder after you announced your wish of building the Mexican border wall and started an investigation against you. For two years, you and Sarah

Sanders endured the press attack that through selected guests, remarked continually the wish of impeaching you.

The firm character of Sarah Sander was crucial to stop those furious journalists who felt have lost the hen of the golden eggs. She was decided to defend you and made it cleverly. Sarah made all the constant press's rude headlines seem normal political matters that you and justice would resolve. Also to further cool the political issues, Sanders pushed the press away from the White House providing short and sharp answers even reducing the traditional press conference by 90 percent. So the media became Sanders's enemy and accused her of lying, but the lies mentioned by the media were just general statements that seem to be more language mistakes than lies.

Mr. President, the two years of Sarah Sander working with you has to be realized as important because Americans could understand how the press act dishonestly, confirming your words, "fake news are the enemy of people". Journalists have always acted partially, defending some and attacking others; journalists invite to their shows selected guests and direct their questions towards attacking opponents and forming fake reputations. Journalists seem to be judges who decide people's fate. Mr. President, it is time to teach the press to be responsible. The press said that the first amendment assures them press freedom but they have to gain freedom by being responsible.

GEMINI BIRTHDAY

June 18, 2019

Mr. President, today Friday, June 14. I wish you a happy birthday. You are now 73 years old. I think you don't count now your years so you don't imagine how heavy the cake could be, but I think you make the years count to continue to achieve more future victories. Many triumphs have been achieved during your whole life but I believe the most important was to become the 45th president of the US. Being president of one of the most powerful countries is truly an honor; but I try to guess why you waited until now to be president and why you wanted to be president, understanding the many difficulties to manage the country.

I said I wanted to guess about your wish to be president because I am like you from Geminis, a fascinating sign that demands perfection and is discovering new things. If you weren't president, you would be enjoying wealth, family, and business work. But not, you are president now facing many problems, attacks, enemies, and diverse situations; that was the dream you wanted to live because that is your personality and your fate. Your twin, active, and exploring personality was shaped by the day and year you were born. From the Chinese record, you have the character of the dog which shows similarities with the western record, Geminis.

Mr. President, you could not be in the house just resting watching tv because although you love family it would be boring for you and there is nothing more unpleasant than a bored Geminis. You have been thinking about being president for a long time but haven't decided to campaign because you needed to know that you would win. You love to be a winner and you would make anything to get what you want. Defeat frustrates, makes sad, and depressed you but you are a brave dog who never gives up.

You also wanted to be president because you are an altruistic person who wants to help the country decisively. Before being president, you suffered a lot observing how the country's crucial problems were never resolved. Different than any other president, in just two years, you did many things and face problems that past administrations avoided to face for fear to be a political failure. For example, the chaos in immigration, the deep incursion of China, tax regulation, faced North Korea, Iran, Isis, improved justice, and looked for peace in the Middle East.

Your commitment has created egoisms that is why Democrats want to impeach you. You are not afraid of anything, you want to continue, and to be reelected because your nature is serving others honestly. My birthday gift is a piece of advice for you: belief in your altruist nature, do what is right, don't believe in polls just continue working, and tell Americans honestly about you, describing your weaknesses and strengths. They will understand you and vote for you.

ANGRY AND GERMAPHOBE

June 20, 2019

Mr. President, there is the belief that you are a bad-tempered person, if so, you must control it because it affects more who feels it than who receives it. Americans may read in different ways your decision of asking the acting chief of staff Mick Mulvaney to leave the room where you were performing a news interview because he coughed. Some may agree with your decision and others not. To perform an interview is hard work and it could be repeated if something goes wrong. Therefore, everyone there must cooperate for the interview to be successful especially Mr. Mulvaney who must know that detail, and as chief of staff should act more carefully as he knows you are a germaphobe person.

Many may also criticize you for reprimanding him in front of everyone. No one wants to be rebuked in front of others and later this episode becomes news. Maybe Mr. Mulvaney and some Americans are detesting you now for Mulvaney's reprimand that you could have managed differently just by stopping the interview and calling Mr. Mulvaney separately. I think Mr. Mulvaney deserves an apology.

At this point when the presidential campaign has started is important not to lose votes by situations that you may avoid or handle better. I know most Americans like your speech because it has not false rules and criticizes openly the traditional politicians who have always acted with hypocrisy. This honest way of acting gives you votes but you can also gain votes by showing respect to your close associates and also by describing to Americans your deepest personal concerns. They will understand you, they would like to know more about your germaphobia and appreciate your effort to be surrounded by many people having to shake hands with them. Please, try to think before speaking and to apply humor.

POLLS DIRECT PEOPLE'S MIND

June 22, 2019

Mr. President, the poll should not be a substitute for thought, said the American philanthropist Warren Buffett, and it should be so because people should vote freely without manipulation. 16

months left for the presidential election, and from now the media seems to know who is going to be the winner and the loser. For them, you are the loser, and Biden or Sanders will win. The media bases its affirmation on surveys elaborated by responsible enterprises with a lot of experience. Americans or people like me who live overseas after reading the poll result start to believe that you will be the loser and Democrats the winners. It seems the media from now starts to adjust people's minds to accept a result coming from an elaborated survey. Mr. President, I think conducting people's minds from a survey is dishonest and you have to act to change that phenomenon.

Understandably, surveys are news because provide information but using it to decide the fate of someone is fake news because the poll is an attempt at describing the feelings of a small population. The survey is like an experiment that can work out or not. The survey data, sources, and information are reliable because they are people's testimony and the survey is elaborated by known companies. However, the poll prediction is not certain because it is just the testimony of a few people who cannot represent totally the reality, and also the poll cannot predict if the present may change.

The media knows the survey is just a prediction that cannot be taken for granted totally; however, it is taken for granted applying a language that discredits who registers low marks and it honors who has the high mark. In the end, many people believe they have to vote for whom the media has been commenting on is better. The media perform like that because is not partial; it is owned by elites who have a close relationship with some political candidate. The 2016 campaign could have been an example because the surveys showed Hillary Clinton above and the media remarked it frequently adding that you (Trump) had a lack of political experience, also were racialists, fascists, and was not able to handle the county. However, you overcame polls and the media comments.

The media seems to want to apply now the same tactics used in 2016 conducting voters. You also could use the same strategy by attacking opponents, although the 2020 campaign is different because it is reelection and you have to show results over the first four years. According to data, 76 percent of the candidates reelected previously had shown good economic results except for president Hoover, Carter, and Bush. Mr. President, you have in this reelection the chance to demonstrate that surveys are predictions that can be overcome, to govern a country suitably you don't need to have political experience it is just necessary to have character and to have the human sense to develop a social and economic plan.

SPONTANEOUS CHARACTER IS WHAT COUNTS

June 24, 2019

Mr. President, you have an immovable character that would be easier to break through steel than your convictions. I think you will win the reelection even though sixteen months before the contest polls are affirming that you will lose. You don't need to worry about polls because the same phenomenon happened with Ronal Reagan and Barak Obama who for the same epoch were 50 percent below. Polls gave Hillary Clinton the winner but they were totally wrong. The main thing that is going to make you a winner is your intense character that brought a new and strong air to

American politics. Your decisive character announcing different ideas and goals was what defeated Hillary Clinton who showed nothing new and now Biden is alike, showing nothing different.

Reagan and Obama were reelected because they had political accomplishments and especially by the distinctive character that Americans seen in them. Regan was always gentlemanly, calm, with style and a large smile. Although Regan made jokes, Obama will be remembered because he liked and enjoyed telling jokes. Everywhere, Obama told a funny remark. The eight years of Obama administration ended up telling jokes and wishing to finish fast because his politics was exhausted, was over, without anything new to show. Hillary Clinton inherited Obama's empty and exhausted policy and started the 2016 campaign without showing a clear political map, but indicating that the elite status quo will continue. Biden is now showing the same: lack of new ideas and opts for preserving the status quo.

Mr. President, instead with your decisive character, you put the status quo upside down, broke all social and political molds, and brought faith to people who had no voice, support with the slogan "make America great again". People screamed after hearing your ideas about creating millions of jobs, building a border wall paid by Mexico, attacking all kinds of opponents rudely; so you won the presidency. Americans voted for you and didn't care about your tax finances, your rudeness, or women's complaints about misconduct. Americans really wanted new ideas. Now you're going to win the reelection because your government was a serial movie and American people like movies. Obama's movie had no second part but your movie has. Americans want to know what is going to happen in the second part of the film: the border wall, illegal immigrants, the fight between the White House and House of Representatives, and what will be the end of Muller's report and the impeachment against you.

International policy is interesting now and Americans also would like to see its development. There are many serious world issues to solve and some are hotter than others. All international issues seem will find a high climax. Iran, for example, is between starting a conflict or a negotiation. China accepted a trade war but could sign a commercial deal too. North Korea started a romance sharing polite letters with you and it could end positively. The Middle East peace plan looks interesting because Palestinians don't seem to have many options currently. Cuba and Venezuela need to be punished harshly because they don't care about people's fate. Mr. President, the need to see the second part of the film is what will win you re-election.

RESPECT THE HATCH ACT

June 27, 2019

Mr. President, it is true that you have many enemies, but I think that between enemies there must be rules of respect. I think it is important to solve the problem that arose this week about the Hatch Act. A federal agency asked you to fire Ms. Kellyanne Conway, a senior counselor, for violating the Hatch Act repeatedly however, you supported her by saying won't fire her. As it has been considered a grave violation of the constitution, House Democrats have subpoenaed Ms. Conway to testify about several accusations related to the violation of the act. This week your daughter Ivanka was also accused of sending public messages supporting you through an electronic server. Also, your son in law, Mr. Kutchner, is been observed by federal agents for the same problem.

Democrats seem to want to make obey the content of the Hatch Act especially at this moment when the political campaign has started. They want to protect their candidates from the influence of government discourse. Mr. President, in this case, Democrats are acting correctly because the power is in your hands currently and you could use it to attack opponents and win the campaign conveniently. The Hatch Act gives you and the Vice president the authority to attack opponents but it limits federal workers to make a partisan campaign. I think the Act's purpose is fair because the opposition candidate may lose easily if you use the machinery of the administration to campaign in your favor.

Mr. President, I think you don't need to worry about the subpoena against Ms. Conway because Democrats will lose it. The Hatch Act is considered right but it is confusing because it authorizes the president's counselors to support the president during his campaign but the aid limits are not clear. So your daughter Ivanka, Ivanka's husband, Mr. Kushner, and Ms. Conway are protected because the norm is not clear. But you could be fair with your opponents by telling your federal workers to refrain from making political comments and leave all comments for you and the Vice president. By acting like this, the idea that you don't respect the constitution could disappear and many more Americans will vote for you.

MUELLER CAN SCARE YOU

June 28, 2019

Mr. President, July 17 will be an interesting day because Mr. Robert Mueller will speak in the House of Representatives about the findings of the investigation against you and he could provide additional information contradicting the exoneration letter sent by Mr. Barr, the Attorney General. Mr. Mueller probably doesn't want to be seen as wasting time investigating and he will disagree with Mr. Barr's letter by remarking your guilt. From now on, you want to defend Mr. Barr's decision and the country from information that may affect its security. You demanded executive privileges to not release some portion of Mr. Mueller's redacted report and ordered your staff to ignore the House subpoena. With this measure, the House knows you want to protect yourself, but Democrats will expect to receive on July 17 first-hand and credible information that may discredit Mr. Barr's letter.

House Democrats won't really need Mueller's report neither the presidency staff testimony because Mueller and his staff are going to clarify any doubt. Mueller and his staff made the investigation against you and both are going to complement what nobody knows. Mr. President, I think you have to be prepared to respond suitably because may emerge unreported evidence, fresh data, new reflections, and conclusions. This phenomenon could happen because Mueller and his staff showed disagreement with the conclusion made by William Barr, the Attorney General. Some of Muller's staff disagree with Mr. Barr's exoneration of you because they think the investigation has clear data that proves you obstructed justice and conspired.

Mr. President, you can take some routes to defend yourself that can be consistent to respond appropriately. The first route is affirming you have never obstructed justice instead you supported justice for two years with federal resources and witnesses to elaborate and finish the investigation against you. The investigation was developed broadly for two years and it concluded you are innocent. The second route is you never conspired with Russia to win the 2016 election. In this route, you may affirm there are language mistakes, misunderstanding and the election rules are not clear because they don't specify exactly the kind of aid a candidate may receive from a foreign country.

NEGOTIATE WITH TREAT

July 1, 2019

Mr. President, when it is threatened directly it cannot be vacillated and actions must be decisive. The threat is a good tool used to negotiate but it is important to be ready for the opponent's response. The opponent's response must be what you are expecting to get and in your case, you need to get everything to make America great again. If you have clear your goal you can get much more from the threat. However, in the threat of rising tariffs to Mexico if this country doesn't control its border to prevent illegal crossing, you gave the impression of being pressed by showing success from negotiation than getting more from.

You announced quickly that Mexico had opted for protecting the border instead of assuming a penalty. In my opinion, you could have gotten much more from that business because the US has more than 30 years of assuming illegals and all kinds of crimes from Mexico as illegal drugs, weapons, and money laundering. You could have asked the president of Mexico, Mr. Manuel Lopez Obrador to build both countries the wall putting a tax on allowances or the transit of vehicles between borders. Involving Mexico in this construction was a promise of the campaign and at that moment, Americans received the idea pleased.

In the G-20 meeting in Japan negotiating the trade deal with China, you gave also the impression you needed the deal more than China because gave many concessions. Before the G-20 summit, you had threatened China by raising trade tariffs and banning Huawei to make business in the US. But you suspended the threat in Japan, canceled raising the tariffs, and permitted Huawei to work again. Maybe you backed down this threat because are thinking about the 2020 reelection and you need farmers' vote who want China to buy more farm products. However, I think you could have gotten more from it if had been more descriptive about Huawei's dishonest business that has been affecting the security and progress of the US.

Mr. President, you have realized that the threats work out well but you have to use them on time and wisely especially against China and communist countries that have gotten much more from the US and other counties. You have to negotiate the threat without giving too many concessions because communism is expanding greatly. Venezuela is an example, North Korea is another that got those lands and they will not return them instead are looking for more strategic lands to colonize. I think the communist colonialism has to be the main reason to use wisely the threat because they are not worried about political election or reelection, they are a single government without parties, so they have enough time to wait until a kindly US president be elected who can give them all they ask.

PATIENT ROLE WITH NORTH KOREA

July 3, 2019

Mr. President, I think you shouldn't trust communism one bit because it is a form of government with a permanent tyrant. You met the North Korean leader on the South Korean border and It was registered everywhere as a historic moment for being the first US president to visit this communist country. However, this matter has been losing interest because there is not any solution and the media now think your presence in North Korea had a political interest. This action, of course, gives you some credibility over leading international issues but you can get more credibility if ask the North Korean leader directly to give peace to the world by accepting a denuclearization process and reunify Korea.

I think you believe you can get a deal with Mr. Kim Jong-un by making a friendship but also could think that it would be a waste of time. Mr. President, North Korea is a communist country and like all of them doesn't care about friendship, doesn't want to make deals with capitalists, and has no word. Communists just believe in their autocratic, repressive, and exploitative philosophy. Mr. Kim is accepting your invitation to see how much gains he can get but then doesn't care anything. Cuba or Venezuela are clear examples of this: Cuba got benefits from the Obama administration but it didn't care for took away those advantages. Venezuela also had many international meetings to solve its crisis but after getting what it needed disappeared without giving explanations. The same could happen to you and again there will be no agreement of peace.

Mr. President, in order this historical moment doesn't end in another failure it is important Mr. Kim Jong-un may understand well the condition to close North Korea's sanctions. I think you may achieve the unification of North Korea and its denuclearization. You can start with the denuclearization plan which needs to be fulfilled gradually until getting the end line. Sanctions are going to be diminished after a verification team confirms that North Korea has reduced effectively its nuclear weapons. You could also reserve some sanction portion to pressure the reunification. Korea really deserves to be reunified now because it has been more than 60 years since the country was divided affecting its culture, family, and nationality. Mr. President, if you may achieve Korea's peace, history could not erase your name, history has to register you as a man who believed in friendship and visions.

FAMILY HELP IS IMPORTANT

July 5, 2019

Mr. President, any battle you can win with the support of the family. You have a large family that seems to be well integrated and supports each other sincerely. You have taken two members of them who probably you love and trust very much to help you to lead the presidency successfully. They are Ivanka, your daughter, and Mr. Kushner, the son in law. They are personal adviser on different matters that are very important for the control of the White House environment and on political issues. You need trustworthy counselors and who better than your family. However, the media and Democrats have criticized that calling it nepotism because you have employed the family; and also they have refused it because consider Ivanka and Mr. Kushner don't have political experience, either background as a diplomatic and political adviser.

They are really doing tasks that demand political experience, and they have no experience. You also have no experience in politics but you are doing a great job as president. Experience in politics is not necessary to work in, it is just important to have common sense, life experience, and educational background and wish to work honestly. You and your family have a lot of those requests, so everything will be achieved successfully. The experience in politics, unfortunately, has been used lately to mask everything, to speak more than work, to delay the progress, and to preserve an elite. The bad work of politics has been proven after you became president because you are speaking sincerely. You said there was a selected group united to the corrupt press who wanted to be in power forever; there was a corrupt and inefficient immigration system, besides the country's infrastructure was abandoned everywhere.

Politics was stagnant and got boring but you brought fresh air and hope. Previous administrations offered problems without showing changes: same wages, high unemployment, drug business everywhere, high crime rates, illegal immigrants everywhere, expensive and discriminatory medical service, homeless everywhere, and old infrastructure. Politicians have also permitted other countries to take advantage of the United States dishonestly without consequences. Mr. President, I understand why you needed your daughter and son in law close to you: you need help to handle the rude and unfair opposition, you need help taking care your back, to give to politics a fresh air and new look, and to help to achieve your vision of making America great again. I see Ivanka and Mr. Kushner as the extra eyes and ears you needed and I think in your position any president would do the same; trust in your family.

THE CELEBRATION OF INDEPENDENCE DAY WAS AN INDEPENDENCE

July 7, 2019

Mr. President, as president you left in the celebration of Independence Day your brilliance, elegance, and power. The celebration of Independence Day was different and interesting, performing new, different, and diverse gala. Your speech was interesting, focused on the country and its history that should always be the center of the celebration. The celebration also increased American's patriotism with the diverse and beautiful anthems, people could take pictures together with the family near to the war tanks, the show of the air force with its planes flying through the sky was great, the extensive parade that represents what the country means was beautiful, the music performed by Carole King, Vanessa Williams, Colbie Caillat and the National Symphony Orchestra was charming. And the celebration closed spectacularly with the colorful firework that was launched from Potomac Park and was visible everywhere.

However, not all people could enjoy the show or feel it really because not all the media covered the event, and days before the event, the media began to distort everything. On July 4th I was in Seoul, Korea, and I had to read many different newspapers and watch images from different channels to understand what was happening. The media had already prepared my mind to understand the celebration as one of your political moves, thinking about the reelection campaign. That you were also trying to politicize the military force putting them as part of the show. That your speech was going to be partisan; that you should not salute the country on that day because you conspired with Russia. That the celebration was going to cost a lot of money. In that way, the media created doubts, fears, and a lack of patriotism about the event.

Mr. President, this episode lets see people how the media acts badly. The media must be impartial but it is not; it is conducting people's minds toward its business interest by attacking who doesn't follow its ideas. It is not objective, makes judgments, it is partisan, defending Democrats and hating you largely. The media had not analyzed your patriotic speech, the successful celebration, and its cost because it is not interested in facts and less in promoting you. The media end ignoring you because it judged you, considering you conspired with Russia to win the presidency. I think what the media did on July 4th was a crime that should be punished because it promoted a lack of patriotism, hatred, lies, fear, doubts, and division.

THERESA MAY GAVE UP BUT YOU DIDN'T, THAT IS THE DIFFERENCE

July 9, 2019

Mr. President, A Chinese proverb says that it is easier to dodge a lance than a hidden knife, and now the knife was in the hands of Theresa May, UK Prime Minister. The news says today that some memos written by a UK ambassador in 2017 given bad references of you were leaked now that the Prime Minister, Theresa May, is leaving office. It is not a coincidence that the writings have appeared suddenly; it is a dirt move against you to discredit you. Displaying the memos now is a form of revenge because you were honest stating that Theresa May failed with the Brexit because she didn't listen to British people's wishes of leaving the European Union, as you had recommended. Further, you are been punished for affirming that Mr. Boris Johnson could be a good UK Prime Minister. But this incident could be also seen as a dirty foreign move made by Democrats who look for any way to discredit you. It is hard to establish how much effort Democrats have done to convince the UK's ambassador to release the memos, but we'll see the truth in the future.

The memos written by the UK ambassador to the US, Kim Darroch, affirm that you are inept and dysfunctional. This means that you are an incompetent person who cannot operate properly. However, this raises a question, who can be more inept and dysfunctional, Theresa May, or you? It is important to clarify that the memos are the UK's government voice because Theresa May has said she supports the ambassador's memos, so she agrees with the ambassador's ideas. Theresa May believes you are a disaster; however, her three years as UK's Prime Minister was a total disaster. Theresa May is not a leader; she couldn't find the unity of her party, the Conservative; no one believed in her because she suggested to fallow different transactions between the UK and the EU. She wasted three years and couldn't achieve the Brexit which UK's people ordered through the 2016 referendum to separate from the EU. Additionally, she was unpopular because the country had some tragic episodes that were handled badly.

Mr. President, Theresa May gave up but you didn't although you have faced worse problems. A person cannot be called inept after suffering two years of investigation with the press attacking every day irrationally. You survived the media ferocity with 44 percent of popularity that no other president could have endured; for that, you should be called a hero. Maybe you were called dysfunctional because you have shown grave problems about Democrats that they want to hide. For example, the border with Mexico and immigration procedures have been managed wrongly. Also, some countries have abused the US's generosity and no one has said or done anything, but you did. The internal and foreign policy doesn't want to see a non-experience person teaching them politics. You have demonstrated to Americans that you are not inept nor dysfunctional, instead have shown character, honesty, and common sense.

CENSUS AND FEAR

July 16, 2019

Mr. President, you are a leader who must cultivate the trust of the entire population. A population census is very important now that the presidential election is near. However, it is confused why you want to include on the census a question asking if he or she is an American citizen or not. It isn't also explicit why Democrats and the Supreme Court don't want to include the question. Additionally, the media's role is to guide people but journalists don't investigate anything, making everything more confusing. Counting people should be an essential matter everywhere and shouldn't be a partisan topic, but it became a partisan political matter and it is used to attack you even when Americans want the question to be included. Mr. President, the question has to be included creating a motivating strategy because people who aren't citizen out of fear they won't fill out the census format.

The question added in the 2020 census will allow people to understand the country more, and Americans will appreciate your effort to defend it. The polemic about the census came because there isn't clear data in the country and people have long been created with false information. The census is developed every ten years in the US and normally after ten years everything has changed, so it is necessary to count the people and know their personal history. Nobody knows exactly how many people are citizens and how many illegals live in the country. The precise census information is important to allocate resources to every state effectively but taking into account that resources have been allocated unequally for 50 years. Unequally is the main reason polls have shown that minorities like Latino migrants, African Americans, and ethnicities want the question to be added.

Democrats may be thinking you want to affect the Electoral College vote number for the 2020 election by adding the question in the census. And the Supreme Court may be thinking not to support the question because it has a political interest. All that may be true but in general, the census data will modify the resources each state is receiving currently. Democrats started to fight hard to avoid the census question by questioning your judgment and affirming you will affect minorities by shortening their resources.

Mr. President, the 2020 census needs to be successful to show it has the most credible data after 50 years. But it could be a failure if the census information is not given by everyone. Illegal immigrants may avoid filling out the census format because may be thinking they will be punished for being illegal. To avoid that misunderstood it is important to design an immigrant strategy that gives them confidence. The strategy will be like a deal in which the illegal's situation will be studied and later he can get partial citizenship. After four years, the illegal can also get total citizenship if he has behaved well. In this way, I think you can be fair with illegal immigrants who have been living for a long time under that condition in the US.

MUELLER DISAPPOINTED

July 28, 2019

Mr. President, now that Robert Mueller has spoken I don't know if you should continue to be risky or cautious; I know that being too cautious little is achieved, so I vote for you to continue being risky. I think Robert Mueller's presentation in the Judiciary House on Wednesday was a disgrace for Democrats and everyone who expected a bombshell. Mueller didn't provide new data either other affirmations that can motivate Democrats to impeach you. Democrats may feel disappointed now and understand there aren't many weapons to fight against you. However, Democrats won't give up to find new data and other ways to accuse you. That is why you have to govern very carefully and don't provide additional information, especially about your finances. To fight against you, Democrats may indict you in courts like the one in New York which works independently about misconducts, government malfunction, and wrong management of your finances. So impeaching could be one legal weapon used against you, but indictment in courts could be used in the future especially when leaving the office.

POLITICIANS, BE GRATEFUL

July 29, 2019

Mr. President, those who criticize the United State is because they will never see something better in their country. Something that wasn't a political strategy became like a good strategy after saying to fresh lawmakers to stop criticizing the US and instead should come back to their root countries to help there. Your words created enormous controversy for several days and the media, as always happens, ended distorting everything. The media affirmed your words generated a xenophobic and intolerant environment in the country. Nevertheless, I think your message hadn't the intention of creating intolerance instead that intended to attract the attention of fresh lawmakers who have received everything from the US and believe they know everything. You suggested that if they know about everything they should go back to their natural country where there are many necessities and help them.

The media created a polemic about it that ended being like a political strategy that favored you. This polemic divided people's opinion about nationalism, making America great again and illegal immigration. Of course, Americans want to protect their citizens, the country, borders, and make America great again. Many more Americans will support the idea of making America for Americans and they are going to vote for that idea in the 2020 election. Mr. President, I think you have added more votes for the next election but also are creating the idea that instead of supporting illegals is better to have a clear, fair, and responsible immigration process.

INTERNATIONAL ORGANIZATIONS DO NOT SERVE

July 30, 2019

Mr. President, compassion is not a luxury or power, it is a basic need that humanity cannot survive without. It is deadly for humanity to have no compassion. Venezuela's crisis has demonstrated that human compassion no longer exists or if there is a little that's hypocrisy. More than five million Venezuelan refugees are trying to survive in other countries because the communist government converted the country to one of the poorest in the world. Anyone who has suffered poverty and injustice in his life could understand how difficult is to be forced to abandon his country, roots, culture with all the family, life, with few bugs. There are few people with compassion who can put in the shoes of the Venezuelans to understand their anguish. For example, International organisms like ONU, OEA or human right defenders are useless because cannot solve anything and they are the bourgeois elite who are only worried about their own economic resources. Communism has also shown that doesn't care about people; it is just interested in keeping Venezuela's territory. Besides, Democratic countries have shown that for them it is more important to think about sanctions, accusations, lies, and wars than protect people immediately.

I think the world is upside down because it preferred insensitivity and hatred. Mr. President, to straighten the world it is necessary to return to principles with which countries were founded like freedom, right to life, equality, citizenship, respect, and tolerance. Venezuela's crisis has more than ten years and no one has shown their leadership and compassion to solve it. You have a great chance to solve the Venezuela crisis by demanding to Venezuela's government respect and support for their citizens. I think economic sanctions are not the solution because they are affecting the country, people including children and old people who have nothing to eat. The solution is a dialog with the government of Venezuela so it commits itself to bring back people to the country and give them all their supplies. Mr. President, it is important to ask Venezuela's president for immediate protection for the population.

YOU ARE DIFFERENT THAN BARACK OBAMA

August 4, 2019

Mr. President, people only trust a man of character, and that's the big difference between you and Obama. After the resignation of the UK's ambassador in the US, Kim Darroch, there is something you need to explain and it is about what Darroch affirmed in his memos. In one memo Darroch affirmed you ended the Obama nuclear agreement with Iran because you wanted to spit the former president Barack Obama. It seems obvious you wanted to affect Obama's image because you ended other important actions made by Obama as the agreement with Cuba, the Obama Health Care, and suspended the annual dinner ceremony with the media. Although those records show there is the intention of affecting Obama, I think your intention was different, and it was to protect the world and the US from Communism, terrorism, unequal health program, and irresponsible media.

The difference between Obama and you is that Obama calculated all his political movements looking for own and future benefits but you don't. You are not a politician that is why you didn't calculate the political cost of your decisions. For example, you decided not to hold the annual press dinner that was almost a ritual in the US, and for this, you could win many enemies in the media. Obama instead had all the press in his hand because he allowed the press to do and say all they wanted, and the media was also happy with Obama because he was the clown at the annual dinner. You also ended the Obama healthcare program that could have brought you many opponents. Obama wanted to be always remembered for this achievement, but Obama's Care Act showed more inconsistencies than benefits. With Obama, everyone couldn't get medical benefits because it demanded to have insurance which included taxes in the medical bill, so Obama's Care turned out expensive and everybody couldn't afford it.

Finishing agreements such as Iran or Cuba was a sensitive issue because the whole international community has supported those. These breakups were a high diplomatic and political risk but you didn't consider that because you saw those deals were putting the world at risk. Communist and fanatic always sign agreements but use this to develop nuclear programs without any permission also use agreements to introduce communism to more countries. Those countries' natures is treacherous and after the betrayal, they deny everything, Communist and fanatic countries are not in rush to win, they can wait patiently until a kind president appears and may give them all that they want. Barak Obama and his vice president, Joe Biden, gave them especially China too many opportunities and they took advantage of it. Thanks to Obama's generosity, China is now a powerful country and goes with the power to conquer the world.

Mr. President, ending those deals may be seen as a spit to Obama but the important is that no one can act weakly against communism. Communist countries have already gained power and space supported by China and Russia. Venezuela is a sad example because it is a rich country located well strategically and was taken by communism. I think Venezuela won't come back to Democrats' hands again because communists are going to fight to the death to preserve the country. Mr. President, what you did is right because you are not a politician who wants to gain popularity, you just want to do the right thing especially to defend freedom and Democracy.

GUNS AND THE RED FLAG

August 7, 2019

Mr. President, the issue of weapons in the United States needs prudence that's why it should be studied well; with prudence, many past evils can be avoided. Now the fake news, Democrat lawmakers and your enemies have found an easy way to determine that you are guilty of the shooting in Texas and Ohio. They have affirmed that you have racist messages and it created a violent environment in the country that caused Texas and Ohio's assaults. That accusation is irresponsible and simplistic because it hasn't evaluated the social background. Gun assaults could have more serious causes in the violence of the country than a message given by you. The causes of violence are several but they need to be found in the whole community that became ill mentally for several reasons as illegal drug consumption, 24 hours of violent images, all kinds of guns everywhere, many poor people, and a chaotic society.

Racist messages aren't really the cause of assaults with weapons in the US. If racist messages had been the cause of it Barack Obama's administration hadn't had deadly assaults because Obama avoided pronouncing racist statements and Obama was also the first black president who people believed would cure the racist hatred in the US. Even though his administration registered a big number, 32 deadly assaults with weapons happened in Obama's eight years. Mr. President, your messages aren't racists and cannot create hate nor division because those aren't hypocritical, are open addresses to everyone: rich and poor people, all countries, black and white, Democrats and Republicans, and especially the media that have not worked responsible and honestly to make America the best country.

The most real cause of deaths by guns in the US is to have weapons in the wrong hands. It is true, there are a big number of weapons in the wrong hands in the country because for a long time the law has allowed everyone to own guns. Wrong hand means people who are not conscious of the right use of guns as children, criminals, and people who are emotional and mentally sick. Children have taken lately guns from their parents without permission and have used those as they see on television programs, playing as a toy, as police, a superhero, or the role of the enemy. This phenomenon happens because parents forget to shelter guns well and media programs are full of violent images that children believe they can perform too.

There are many cases registered in the US in which children have taken their parents' guns and end killing their family or they go to school and end also killing their classmates. Many cases are also recorded in which fanatics, resentful, frustrated, depress, or mentally sick end shooting people. Those people are conscious of the danger of the weapon but aren't conscious about themselves, becoming potential shooters. But most of these people become potential shooters because the law allows them to own guns without verifying their social or mental background.

Mr. President, the solution to this grave problem that kills many Americans every year is not to put guns in the wrong people. There is a law called the "red flag" that orders gun sellers to verify people's background before selling guns but it hasn't worked properly although this law is from 2005. This law doesn't work accurately due to the whole society has not been integrated to perform the red flag. Authorities don't know who is a potential shooter and people don't inform on time who have those characteristics. To act properly, gun sellers need to have precise data from authorities but they haven't. Accurate information also could be taken from a study-application filled out by the applicant which has to be researched during a period before providing the gun. Mr. President, taking time to study the applicant's background may avoid putting guns in the wrong hands.

FIRE THE SECOND AMENDMENT OR REGULATE IT

August 11, 2019

Mr. President, creating an atmosphere of peace in the world is a correct decision, so the sale of weapons must be regulated to a minimum. You should eliminate the second amendment from the constitution and Americans will thank you a lot. Even if you may achieve it, history will register you as the president who took the most sensible action to protect human life. It may be hard to achieve this because there are a lot of opponents who defend the lucrative business of selling arms to the public. The purpose of the second amendment was people could protect themselves with guns, but it became a lucrative business. The amendment's purpose was enunciated 200 years ago when American society had different concerns, and more violence but the current society is a social chaos that demands more social help, education, piece of advice, health, housing, and education than guns. Mr. President, it is time to end the gun business and to start to restore the society providing all the social facilities, so people can live in peace.

There are many reasons to justify before the Supreme Court the termination of the second amendment. It was performed in 1791 when there was not a strong army and there was also fear the enemy could invade again. So the amendment allowed the creation of militias from the population and to keep and bear arms. Currently, the US has the best military forces in the world that can defend the country perfectly without employing militias. Therefore, armed militias shouldn't exist in the US because there is a legal military force that is the only one who must carry weapons. The amendment also stated that the militia should be well regulated because at that time, justice wasn't well organized and it didn't want people to commit excesses using guns. Justice is now a strong and honorable system in the US and it is the only one that can dictate that individuals cannot make justice by their hands using guns.

Another reason is that the US is chaotic in terms of social order and security. Mr. President, the country is a time bomb that is almost exploding because most of the guns are already in the hands of the people who have serious social problems as business and consumption of drugs; criminal gangs; resentful religious, politicians and immigrants; depressive and mentally ill people. There is also the risk children take up guns by mistake and use them as toys.

What the shooter in Paso, Texas, did was take justice into his own hands; and the shooter in Ohio was mentally sick. Besides both are young with no more than 23 years old, and this shows the negative influence that the media has on them by teaching violence continuously. Mr. President, the second amendment has no helped society at all instead since its proclamation 200 years ago more Americans have died than in wars. That people carry guns never have to be a good idea that is why the majority of countries have banned this except Mexico, Guatemala, and the US. Currently, Mexico and Guatemala are a social mess because there are arms in the wrong hands who want to make their own justice. The US can go in the same way if arms sales to individuals do not stop. I know that it is difficult to eliminate the second amendment because of the appreciation that Americans have for weapons and for the business it represents, but the sale of weapons can be regulated so that they are in the right hands.

THE DANGER OF CONSPIRACY THEORY

August 15, 2019

Mr. President, people are asking life and those who run the world to please stop lying to them; people became mediocre, ignorant, and simplistic because the information from everywhere is fake news. One form of fake news is creating a conspiracy or intrigue. That words themselves indicate that they are born from untruth and are formed in secret to affect anyone especially the government. Conspiracy is not a theory because has lacks accurate data so this affects the way people think. Mr. President, you have given several conspiracy statements and the media has accused you of using those for your benefit. But the media is also informing through intrigues and both are affecting the way people think. Anyway, conspiracy arguments are being used more frequently now by important public officers and media because it is easy to talk without proves, getting a lot of benefits easily but the reality is affected.

No One knows now who, how, and why the most tragic and violent events have happened. There is total ignorance about why President John F. Kennedy was killed; why the twin towers in New York were destroyed; why Iraq was invaded and destroyed if there were not any danger there. Those are some examples of ignorance but there are many: was there a holocaust in Germany really? Have we visited the moon really? People don't know if what they have heard about past episodes were true or false. There is a total absence of reality currently and people have to turn to believe in something. Politicians and media have taken advantage of people's ignorance and have suggested answers about some episodes in the form of intrigue or conspiracy, accusing anyone. In the end, people consider the intrigue reasonable and start to believe in any answer and any person.

The two most recent examples of conspiracy are the one you accused the former President Bill Clinton of being involved in the death of Jeffrey Epstein, an American financer accused of a sex offense, who seams committed suicide in a jail in New York. Mr. President, you affirmed that both, Clinton and Epstein, had a close relationship and Clinton could have participated in Epstein's sex crimes. That information hasn't been confirmed, but there is some proven evidence about and you believe Mr. Clinton ordered to kill Mr. Epstein to erase any connection.

The other example is the conspiracy made against you by the media for two years but there is a difference with Clinton's case and that is that here there is no evidence of a crime. The conspiracy against you started in 2016 when you won the presidency; the media claimed you were incompetent for this work; that you were going to destroy the country; that you conspired with Russia to win the election; that you don't work; that you made fraud at the opening ceremony; that haven't released tax information because you made fraud; that your son in law and your daughter Ivanka are corrupted; that you are racist and hate women. All those statements were announced every day without any verification.

Because this conspiracy that Americans notice is fake news is possible to figure out its outcome that is to form a conflictive and unfair society: a person's reputation is destroyed, resentments are created, people believe about false accusations and so behave; however, the person who has displayed the intrigue gets a social reputation. I think this form of communication has to be stopped and needs to be considered a crime because this can increase resentment. The media and public officers have to be conscious of using fiction to inform because it generates social violence. Mr. President, I know you are conscious about it because you have affirmed you wanted the media to understand how you can feel after being attacked with lies for two years.

SHOPPING GREENLAND IS FUN

August 20, 2019

Mr. President, you are a full dreamer who wants to be in impossible places. Some cartoonists and comedians already started to make fun of your idea of buying Greenland. They have described you playing golf in the middle of Greenland's snow corridor. No one has still said the idea of buying Greenland may be a political move to win the 2020 election, but someone could soon make the announcement. I could be the first one to say that your idea of buying Greenland is more a political move because it is based mainly on making people dream about great and unimaginable things and that you can make Americans dream.

Mr. President, I think Americans had not dreamed again since they went to the moon with the Apollo 11 in 1969 but dreams came back now with your slogan about making America great again. Having a functional border wall with Mexico and now buying a foreign country island that is twice bigger than Texas with abundant natural resources and located strategically to control Europe and Asia means to dream again. Buying Greenland was thought before by other administrations but bringing this issue again is important because Americans start to believe again about themselves, their country, and that they can achieve anything.

Americans are dreaming again and they do it like when they met their superheroes in the movies. Mr. President, you created this phenomenon of dreaming again. To dream is more important than anything else and for this, Americans surely are thankful and are going to reelect you in the next contest. You know it is impossible to buy Greenland. Denmark's government has already said the Island is not on sale, but Americans don't care about the negative answer they care more about the person who makes them dream. Americans need you to dream: they already believe the economy will be the best with abundant job opportunities and high salaries. Also, they will have the safest and private country thanks to a strong border wall. Taxation will be also fair as well as the health system. Besides, Americans may believe they will have more control over the world. They don't know how much of those ideas are true or fantasy but what Americans want is to dream.

REPUBLICANS REALLY SUPPORT JEWS

August 23, 2019

Mr. President, if you help just a person or an important cause such as Israel and Palestine, you have not lived in vain, Martin Luther King advised. Everyone needs to understand that your last announcement looks for unity instead of anti-Semitism. You affirmed that Jews who vote for Democrats have a lack of knowledge and are disloyal. In other words, you suggest that Jews who vote Republicans have the knowledge and are loyal. This statement seems to look for preferences and division but it is not; instead, it is a great lesson about respect, tolerance, and love. This episode reminds Jews that they cannot forget the anti-Semitic history have suffered but also that at this time, just Republicans are supporting the Jews promoting peace in the region, putting Israel as leader of the region, trying to provide a better life for Palestinians and constructing friendship between Palestinian and Jews.

Jews need to remember that no one help them when they were exterminated, that you have not forgotten that heartbreaking episode and want to support them. Throughout history, the Jews have been exterminated and they themselves have risen from the ashes without help because it is a united and strong culture. Selfishness may have been the main reason to kill Jews because they are smart folk who have provided great ideas to improve society and the world. Jews were killed because they understood religion in a different way than Christians, and Hitler also ordered killed them because considered they have gotten a lot of power in society and could govern it. However, the Jewish race was not exterminated and this is a powerful population that wants the sad history doesn't repeat itself.

Asking not to vote for Democrats can be seen as a way of saying vote for me, but it is not. It is a form of saying Democrats don't deserve Jews to vote for them because Democrats haven't done any real thing to solve Israel's problem and problems between Palestinians and Jewish. Previous US administrations have governed but none had a real plan to give peace to the region. Those administrations have felt comfortable doing nothing, letting time pass, and always taking this problem as a strategy for political campaigns. While you try to promote peace in the region, two Democrats representatives, Somali-American Minnesota Representative Ilhan Omar, and Palestinian-American Rashida Tlaib are doing the opposite creating hate.

Mr. President, when you affirmed additionally that Jews who vote for Democrats are disloyal it is because they don't realize how much you have done to make Israel a more powerful country. You declared Jerusalem as the capital of Israel, you moved the US embassy to Jerusalem, and have declared Gaza's territories property of Israel. These decisions have a political cost and have made you win enemies but it had to be done to make Jews stronger so that a holocaust is avoided again. Also, it had to be done to provide order in the region and so begin a peace plan. Mr. President, you designed a peace plan for the region accompanied by Mr. Kushner, your son in law, which so far has been rejected by Palestinians although the plan was very generous, suggesting 50 billion to build a better society in Palestine.

Mr. President, most of your predecessors affirmed that they wanted peace in Israel but they didn't do anything effective to achieve it. You have assumed the role of peacemaker, have taken huge risks and everything has been done honestly and effectively. All the actions done by you have been a bomb, including your last statement asking Jews not to vote for Democrats. But more than being a bombshell, your actions show courage, these don't have a personal interest and are more a demonstration of generosity and love.

IN G-7 YOU SHOW WHO YOU ARE

August 27, 2019

Mr. President, in the midst of all the difficulties that exist in the world and that you have, opportunities will appear. You showed confidence and enough knowledge by responding correctly at the press conference that closed the G 7 summit. I think you were the main protagonist of G 7's conference although other leaders wanted to see you as a loser. For example, French President Emmanuel Macron wanted to be the principal character of the meeting, producing unexpected news. Macron invited Iran's Foreign Minister to come to the summit, thus disapproving of the sanction that you put on Iran. However, you didn't give too much attention to Macron's disloyalty but responded smartly that Iran is a serious problem and needs more talks. Instead, you developed there your prepared agenda that was about business mainly and in the end, you got more than you were looking for, demonstrating that you were not waiting for surveys but to help the country.

You stepped in the earth with fire because the EU was where the main concern was, and it was about the trade rates. In the G 7 summit, you had to do the work that past administrations had not done that was to set the appropriate commercial rates. The same problem was happening with China who took advantage for 30 years of the negligence and kindness of past administrations and now the negotiation became a trade war. Fortunately, the EU understands more than China that needs to strengthen the friendship with the US because the economy declines in Europe while the US shows strong numbers. At the end of the summit, you exhibited good empathy and agreements with German's chancellor Angela Merkel and UK's PM, Boris Johnson.

At the same time, the agreement with Japan to buy the excess agricultural products have helped to relieve the trade war with China. You also affirmed gladly China's wish of reopening negotiations. You strongly believed that China could decide to negotiate because its economy has declined, the Communist Party forces the Chinese president, Mr. Xi, to make a decision, and American companies want to leave China. Mr. President, I think that was a good outcome for a two days' summit, although the profit hasn't still concreted. To get that good outcome you have to continue believing that the US is strong enough, that the country has been victimized by China for many years and it has to pay for it. You also need to ask Americans to support you because this process is very unpopular with many difficulties and was bravely assumed by you because previous administrations were negligent.

TRADING STRATEGIES

August 29, 2019

Mr. President, you know that in business you have to take risks because a ship is safe in the port but it was not built for that, commented the writer Paulo Coelho. At the G 7 summit, you made your way of negotiating and handling diplomacy known. You had previously taught your strategy to do business but at the G 7 summit, everybody understood its characteristics. The strategy includes moving forward and backward, say yes and no, throwing compliments and disapprovals, false announcements, reducing supply and leaving the negotiation. You used that negotiation strategy working in the real estate business because that has worked out for you, according to what you have said. That experience was successful in the real estate area but you have to prove now if it works out in politics. So far the signs indicate that your strategy doesn't work very well in politics but it is too early to give a verdict because in the end China and the EU could sign a trade deal or Iran and North Korea could give up to produce nuclear weapons or you could buy Greenland.

The most illustrative episode is the rate negotiation process with China. After announcing that you have increased the commercial tariffs to China, in the G 7 summit you gave compliments to the president of China, saying that he is a great leader but later you also affirmed that China has been cheating the US in billions of dollars for many years. But much later you said you have a second thought about tariffs because president Xi wants to make a deal and the deal could be 50-50, something very generous compared to the high rate that had been announced. Nonetheless, official sources from China have affirmed that the Chinese president has never called to the White House to reopen negotiations.

Mr. President, your strategy in general describes more reversals and the need to sign an agreement. Going back is an important tool in negotiations because can provide a second thought but showing anxiety to get the deal could reduce the negotiation margin. Although calculated anguish can be useful too. If you said 50-50 it means it will be the margin or maybe you consider 45 percent is a good deal too. On the other hand, the strategy used with North Korea has to be different than with Iran. You gave many compliments to the North Korean leader and let him do and say what he wants while Iran was imposed hard economic sanctions. It could have happened because you consider Iran a real threat while North Korea does not.

The panorama now is to wait and see what happens. Maybe the menace, compliments, or the calculated anguish could seduce or force actors to make a deal or not. The menace has worked out on some occasions: for example, President Obama made with Iran a deal in 2014 when Iran was sanctioned. The menace could work out again and Teheran may ask for a deal. China and North Korea instead work differently; they don't accept menaces, they make deals when they see benefits. Those countries don't have the anguish of running presidential elections every four years, so they can wait calmly until another US president can give them what they ask. Mr. President, you cannot expect positive things from China or North Korea; we know they hate the US, capitalism and they won't change that idea. I think you have to act radically against them to stop the abuse of China and the advance of communism in the world.

CLOSE THE G-7

September 1, 2019

Mr. President, it seems that G -7 group is dogma and this makes the country live with the truths of others and not with its own. The G 7 summit described a confusing map between multilateralism and bilateralism, the wrong attitudes of its leaders, and the uncertain future of the group of 7. From the beginning when the summit was taking place, things started badly because the French president, Mr. Macron, invited unilaterally Iran's Foreign Minister, Mr.Zarif, The purpose of this visit was not clear; maybe Mr. Macron planned to be the summit main actor or he wanted to solve the Iran-US issues really. Then you, Mr. President, suggested Russia should return to the G 7 group which was denied by everyone except Italy alleging that before entering, Russia must solve everything about the invasion of Crimea.

This general rejection about including Russia in the G 7 group could suggest diverse interpretations: Word leaders aren't considering you a legal leader because Russia interfered in the 2016 elections; they want to punish you because the trade war with China is affecting everyone; they may be considering that your nationalist inclination is dangerous; also they may want to punish you for isolating yourself from the climate agreement. And your open support to the UK's PM, Boris Johnson saying that you want Johnson to become PM for a long time, teaches that you prefer a divided EU. Later, you made an affirmation that everybody is still trying to understand because that seemed to be a false statement. You said the Chinese president has sent a message saying he wanted to reopen negotiations with the US. With that statement, maybe you wanted to calm down the world market or gain more support in the summit or push president Xi to make a deal; nevertheless, it helped you to end the summit relaxed.

Finally, significant facts are showing that the G7 can dissolve and you, Mr. President, will be the main protagonist of this. For example, the seven counties haven't signed agreements last and this year. Last year because you left the summit before finishing, and this year because there was no agreement on anything. Next Year you will host the G7 leaders and from now on there is discomfort because you already invited president Putin; you also don't want to sign environmental deals, avoid multilateral groups and the next summit could also end without agreements. I think the G7 has no reason to exist; the G20 could replace the G 7 because that has more influence in the world. Mr. President, you have the great historical chance to end the G7 that doesn't represent anything to the world, doesn't provide benefits but does cause huge expenses.

LIFE PRESERVERS FOR AMERICANS COMPANIES IN CHINA

September 4, 2019

Mr. President, voters may be fooled but American companies trying to survive in China cannot be fooled. You initially suggested to American companies to leave China but now you are pressuring them to get out quickly, mentioning the act that orders to abandon a country when there is an economic emergency, (IEEPA). But you know there isn't an economic emergency in the US; maybe you mentioned the IEEPA to pressure China to make a business deal and end the trade war. Mr. President, suggesting or ordering companies leave China may be a bad idea because nothing protects them in the US, China could also order companies leave its country and the companies could be left without bread and cheese.

The IEEPA (International Emergency Economic Powers Act), is the last option used when there is an unusual and real threat against the US' economy, security, or foreign policy. The economy of the US is not at risk currently, on the contrary, it is improving while the rest of the world is in recession. Economic growth was estimated at 1.8 but rose to 2.1 percent. National security and foreign policy aren't also at risk; the US has the most powerful military force around the world, and you are reinforcing the border. I think, for now, the US companies shouldn't leave China because they are going to face many problems.

The main problem the US companies will face is that they cannot find anywhere the big number of consumers that there are in China especially the middle class. Food companies like McDonald's, KFC, and Starbucks have lucrative profits thanks to more than 1000 million Chinese consumers. China's middle class with more than 400 million people keeps business afloat as tech, food, and airlines. The other problem is where those US companies can go if the number is not insignificant. There are more than 80 thousand restaurants and stores of McDonald's, KFC, Starbucks, and Pizza Hut in China. Mr. President, you said those companies can choose to go to another Asian country like the Philippines, Malaysia, Vietnam, Indonesia but the problem is that those markets are saturated with US brands and those countries want to open their own business.

The other thing is that China doesn't need American companies to operate there because China has its own market, the largest number of consumers, and a nationalism that can determine what people should consume. China could force the US companies to leave the country by establishing hard law measures or by making them fail to ask people don't buy the US products. China does not depend on the US market; business between both countries is around 20 percent and China could replace that by looking at other markets. Mr. President, if the US companies leave China they will lose China and will not find support outside. The companies will be abandoned to their fate; that is why the government needs to design a plan to guide, and care for them.

TRADE WAR WITH CHINA IS NECESSARY

September 7, 2019

Mr. President, China does not hate the United States, I think it hates itself because it cannot be like the United States. You started a trade war with China because China has been stealing the US' intellectual property for many years making profits in billions of dollars. Of that profit, the US hasn't received any economic benefits but China has been able to advance very much social, economic, military, and technologically. China is now considered the largest economy and powerful after the US; but for many specialists, China is the most powerful nation around the world. Mr. President, you have realized China's unfair way of progressing for many years and you want to stop that. So this trade war looks like to be the beginning of another cold war led by two men who each defend passionately their philosophy.

This doesn't seem to be a trade war but instead, this looks like a war of powers that could lead to a real war where everyone dies or survive one, or where two nations with different ideology could be accepted by everybody to lead the world. You and Mr. Xi launched the trade war last year in July 2018 when import tariffs were around 3 percent and now are up 20 percent. With this increase, each one is showing their power, none shows fear or respect for the other. You have said it is better to be without China and China has affirmed it can lead its economy well without the US. Both consider are powerful now and also, both consider they have the best political system.

It is true that now both countries are strong but also it is hard to determine who is stronger because China doesn't display sensible information. The US is a developed country for a long time while China has advanced globally very much in the last five decades. Like the US, China has a nuclear arsenal but China's military troop is bigger than that of the US currently. In the economy, the US shows a large distance with China reflected in its GDP per capita above 50 thousand dollars while China barely reaches 10 thousand dollars. However, China will have more economic stability because it has five times more population that represents a huge and cheap economic workforce, being this attractive to many, but this for China is the best capital.

China has accelerated its pace to grow lately and may think it is time to challenge the US. China is not going to stop its growth and the same the US will do, but who can believe and defend their ideology is going to triumph. Capitalism and Communism have been always enemies because one of them wants to rule the world. Democracy has reigned almost everywhere but many people have felt disappointed because Democracy's inequality, violence, and poverty are enormous; however, people have preferred to live in a freedom world than in a controlled regime as the communist is. At this moment when protests are happening in Honk Kong because China wants to interfere in Honk Kong's democracy, people are demonstrating that they prefer democracy to communism. However, Hong Kong's people are going to need more than a protest because president Xi believes that communism is what the world needs.

Mr. President, a war cannot happen to solve the war trade because it will be the destruction of the world. Necessarily the world power will continue divided between communism and capitalism although capitalism will reign everywhere even in communist countries because capitalism allows to move the economy efficiently and easily. In the end, the Chinese president will make a trade deal with you because he understands that China isn't still strong enough and have to work toward that. However, communists never forget their goal of being the world's leaders and they will try to achieve this by taking advantage of capitalist ideas and stealing capitalist's intellectual property.

THE FIRST LADY IS YOUR SUPPORT

September 11, 2019

Mr. President, You know that you and Melania are not a perfect couple, but problems can be overcome together. The media have attacked Melania badly many times and that's why you could change your thoughts about her, and Melania could feel sad and frustrated. About the past of your wife, you know already what was right and wrong and you accepted her with that past. However, the role that Melania has played as the first lady described by the media can make you think that Melania is not the right person to be the first lady of the most powerful nation.

The media has described Melania as the first lady who always acts wrongly. When you took the presidency, the media affirmed that Melania imitative her dress and plagiarized her speech: the pale blue dress from the former first lady Jackie Kennedy and the speech from Barack Obama's wife, Michele Obama. Also, Melania's decision to live in the Trump tower to take care of her young son Barron during the first year of your administration was described as wrong. Melania has also been called the absent first lady because she does not appear in public frequently. The media hate Melania's dress style too, saying it is boring and old fashion. Besides, they have criticized Melania's English accent because it is not an American accent. Lately, the media has implied that you don't like her anymore and that she wants to deceive you because she was pictured giving a loving kiss on the cheek of the Canadian Prime Minister, Mr. Trudeau.

Mr. President, you shouldn't change the noble opinion about your wife taking press information. You, better than no one, know her and also know that she has acted as the first lady correctly. You have been together for a long time: you met Melania almost twenty years ago and you have been married for fourteen years. Melania gave you happiness again providing a beautiful son; and also gave you youth because she is almost twenty years younger than you. Your wife is not perfect but needs to appreciate her bravery. Melania's roots are not from a rich family, she is from a town and immigrated to make the American dream. She achieved many personal goals but fate had her to be the US's first lady.

As the first lady, Melania has been a mother, wife, and faithful company in your ideas, adventures, and trips. She has never been absent of her role; Melania has been working on the program "Be Best" to protect Americans especially youths from drugs and bullying. The first lady has always acted discreetly; Melania's clothes have been suitable for each different event. The messages that she has delivered have been always respectful, it has never tried to be above you or deceive you as the media has affirmed. Mr. President, you have a great woman and the best you can do is protect, improve the relationship, and be happy together.

THE SYSTEM IS INEFFICIENT

September 13, 2019

Mr. President, I think the time to correct mistakes and do things right is now. The serious problem about providing and protecting clean water reveals that there is a complicated way of governing in the US that needs to be modified. That way of governing doesn't allow to solve urgent problems quickly, putting the population at risk of getting sick or die. For this inefficient way of governing, some infrastructures in the US are very old that seems to come from the beginning of the 20 century or belong to an undeveloped country. It is the case of the lead pipes which were installed a long time ago, the corrosion now is contaminating the water, making people sick but the government cannot act quickly to replace these pipes. This problem should be called a national emergency in order the government was able to invest resources to replace the lead pipes around the country.

The other problem is there isn't continuity in the government's work because a president does something and the next president does not continue or cancel that. This lack of continuity in work wastes time and limits the development of the country. There are examples of lack of continuity: Obama's Healthcare, Iran's nuclear pact with President Barack Obama, and the commercial forgiveness of Cuba. The most recent refusal was about protecting streams and wetlands that feed the great water sources from their landowners who are destroying that natural resources. This rule from the former president Obama called Clean Water Act sought that landowners don't build near the water or grow goods using chemicals that may affect the water. This rule and all the other Obama's agreements were fundamental, but you canceled those because considered those projects had weaknesses and needed to be rejected.

Obama's healthcare, for example, demands more costs than benefits; Iran continues improving its nuclear arsenal, and Cuba doesn't still provide freedom to its population. In the case of Obama's Clean Water Act, this is wrong because it was just trying to protect water sources but affects the landowners' economy. Landowners cannot work their lands because they have to protect water. I think it is not the right way of ruling; Obama needed to elaborate a plan which could benefit both, water and landowners. That must have been an environment plan in which the protection of water doesn't affect the economy and economic tasks do not affect water sources. It means that landowners can work their land because they know how to work it without affecting water stores.

There are basically two problems about the way of governing in the US: one is that the government cannot act fast to solve sensible problems. This problem has been illustrated with the lead pipe dilemma which has not been resolved because this will cost more than 30 billion, and those old lead pipes are located mainly in states where poor people live and lawmakers don't care about the health and life of those people. The other problem is that the government's plans do not have continuity from one administration to the other because the plans are not designed correctly. Mr. President, you have the solution on your hands because you have experience with the construction of the border wall with Mexico. The solution is in declaring a national emergency to get resources, doing that, you can demonstrate that governing through Congress is an inefficient form of governing because there are many obstacles to solving urgent problems and plans are rejected because those are bad elaborated due to the political game of interest.

THE UNITED STATES MAKES ISRAEL GREAT

September 16, 2019

Mr. President, the best is not to seek the war between Israel and Palestine but the solidarity so that both nations achieve their objectives. The strategy used to weaken Iran's power and balance forces in the Middle East could arrive at the end if you may sign a more demanding deal than the former President Obama did. A strong and effective agreement could bring peace to the Middle East definitely by weakening Iran, putting Israel as a powerful leader of the region, and the US with more allies and a good relationship with everyone. Israel has been the center of this strategy after it was declared a state, became a strong US ally to gain power over Palestine, and got a white card to attack any territory that unbalances the region, including Iran.

The US relationship with Israel has been very important to Israel because has allowed creating the idea that Israel is a powerful country that may destroy any enemy. That idea may be true or not but it is necessary to be exhibited because the Middle East needs a leader who can stop forms of violence as to build nuclear weapons, support terrorist groups, and make more allies; leadership may bring more democracy, development, and peace to Palestine and the whole region. Previous US presidents have allowed Israel to launch threats against Iran and it may consider attacking Iran unilaterally. That permission gave Israel just confidence but nothing more because the same problems continue. Mr. President, now you are doing what no president did before: you gave more worldwide status to Israel after announcing Jerusalem as the capital of Israel, also that Golan Heights territory belongs to Israel and not far away, Israel can annex Palestine territory of West Bank and Gaza.

Those decisions can be seen as unfair because the UN has declared that no country can annex territories unilaterally. However, what you have done is not unfair because it may bring peace to the region, understanding that the center of the war has been Palestinians' refusal to share the territory with Israel. Palestinians consider the entire territory their property but currently, Palestinians cannot do anything about it because Israel was declared a formal state by the UN. Declaring the state of Israel created chaos because Palestinians refused to create a state, declared war on Israel and Iran decided to support Palestine.

In whole the process of trying to bring peace, Iran has been as the comedian because is a rich country that can support terrorist groups and build a nuclear bomb. But at the same time, Iran has helped indirectly Israel to be a strong state by being the enemy of Israel. Israel with the support of the US has been able to respond to Iran and to become a solid nation. Mr., President, pushing Iran to sign a more demanding deal will force him to not interfere more and not let Iran advance its military. This reality will make Palestine realize that Iran have not strong allies anymore, accept that Israel will be leading the region and that Palestinians need a formal state. Continuing to support Israel openly is the way Palestinians could accept the reality of two countries sharing the region. Mr. President, I think you have figure out the peace will come soon because your son in law, Mr. Kushner, brought the noble idea of supporting Palestine economically with 50 billion to build the country. Or maybe you are thinking that peace demands to make a social plan for Palestine that cost a lot of money. I think financial aid is better than political interference.

THE IMPEACHMENT WILL BE A FAILURE

September 19, 2019

Mr. President, be careful because Democrats want to simulate justice in many ways. There are many reasons to believe the impeachment inquiry against you worked by the Democrat House and the judiciary committee will never be successful and, in the end, you may get great popularity. This is because polls are showing division among the democrats and their numbers are not enough to impeach you; also the Democrat House doesn't have the credibility to achieve the impeachment, and Republicans in Congress are the majority. The Democrat House has to consider that if it starts the impeachment against you it will be seen as a circus where nothing is serious. And if the impeachment process fails, everything is going to works out in your favor, increasing your popularity to win the reelection.

Numbers everywhere are shown disagreement about starting an impeachment process against you. It is known that many Americans hate you, but many more love you, and they don't want you to be impeached. Polls have registered sympathy on you, and, curiously, no all democrats want to impeach you, at least 30 percent of them are against the impeachment. On the Republicans' side, more than 95 percent support you. But the most important is to realize that the inquiry won't progress because the majority are Republicans in congress.

The Democrat House has lost credibility because you have demonstrated that the executive has much more power and the House has made a mediocre performance. You have stopped most of the subpoenas ordered by the House by declaring executive privileges. The House has responded angrily that the president cannot be above the law, but you have demonstrated that you are the governor and the law protects his government. Besides, the House has tried to show its power by opening a parallel investigation to the one made by the special counsel Robert Mueller for two years but it was also a failure. Some witnesses haven't shown up and those who have appeared have declared that they are protected by the president's executive privileges and that do not have to respond to anything. The House at the end has performed like a circus where the show is diverse, funny and people pay for entertainment.

Mr. President, I think you don't have to worry about the accusation because this won't be processed successfully; however, you have to continue working effectively and acting cautiously. So far you have shown audacity by getting what you want and doing what the country needs. Americans will be grateful and continue supporting you because the economy is successful and security is improving. Everyone has seen how much you have fought to build the southern border wall and it is a reality now with more than 200 miles built. Nevertheless, you need to act cautiously because Democrats and the media will continue investigating until they can find something that may stop your reelection. Mr. President, continue refusing to provide any information and continue protecting your finances, that's the best you can do for now.

DOUBLE STANDARDS

September 21, 2019

Mr. President, now that you see so much injustice against you, you must fight with more force. The media and democrats attack their opponents unfairly using lies without mention proof but at the same time, democrats defend their followers hiding the truth. This is the total absence of political ethics. This phenomenon has been proven after you were investigated for conspiracy but former President Obama hasn't been investigated for spying on your campaign. Currently, they consider you guilty without evidence, but they don't mention anything about the previous administration. You were also attacked because declared a national emergency to get cash to build the southern border wall, but Democrats haven't been investigated for doing anything in eight years to solve the immigration problems. And lately, you were accused of pressuring a foreign country to investigate the candidate Biden, but no one wants to know about Biden's abuse of power.

This dual behavior is shaping our society and is going to be dangerous, unfortunately. No one expected you to win but you won the presidency; Democrats and the media didn't accept defeat and started a fierce attack on you. They looked at everything about you and found that you had a connection with Russia before the election and used that to win the presidency. Democrats and the media expected to put you in jail soon accusing you every day of conspiracy. This hasn't happened yet after two years of an investigation against you, but until now no one has investigated the media and Democrats' hostile behavior, neither how they found the information against you nor why there isn't any investigation against Obama, Joe Biden, and Hillary Clinton for doing nothing during eight years of government.

Later, they started to obstruct and discredit your work by saying that you were unable to lead the country and were also called crazy because wanted to build the border with Mexico. The Democrat House and Congress denied money for the border wall, saying a border is something immoral and unnecessary. You persisted in your idea and got funds different from those of the congress. But so far no one has investigated the previous administrations for having abandoned the border where are created all kinds of crimes that enters the US, forming a grave problem of insecurity. Democrats have also accused you of pressuring a foreign country to investigate the presidential candidate Joe Biden. Democrats said it was an abuse of power and it deserves to be impeached, but they haven't mentioned the crimes committed by the former Vice President making business with Ukraine's corrupt company.

Mr. President, the race for the presidency shows that nobody wants to lose and nobody wants to accept defeat. The loser has always a plan B to bring down the winner as being impeached, discredit or accuse of any wrong action. This wrong political behavior is ending with good human manners because the media is giving false information as a true. During the eight years of Obama's presidency, he formed a corrupt elite including the media that ruled for themselves and didn't want to give up power

THE NEED TO BE IMPEACHED

September 25, 2019

Mr. President, it has been seen that you like popularity a lot and have a lot of ingenuity to achieve it as you are doing with the indictment process against you. I think democrats have determined to save their honor impeaching you finally as Nancy Pelosi has announced. The Democrats House has spent more than two years to impeach you and now they have found more motives to proceed. The Democrats added to the special counsel Robert Muller's two years investigation a report that shows you influenced Ukraine's president to investigate Joe Biden, the democrat candidate. Pelosi and her caucus have considered that was an abuse of power's crime as well as the conspiracy with Russia investigated by Muller. Despite this difficult situation, you haven't stopped attacking your opponents, nothing about the impeachment seems to worry you; this seems to be that you are seeking to be accused; maybe, because you have considered the impeachment is convenient for you.

If you are thinking the impeachment process is going to favor you, you are right. The indictment can help you in many ways: that helps you to unite more the Republican Party, Americans and you can save your future by getting reelection. Most Americans, Republicans, and even some Democrats are going to support you because they have seen your decisive character to defend America and make it great again. Everyone knows you have done many more achievements than any other presidents and you have demonstrated that before administrations were ruling for themselves, not for the people. The accusation process is going to make you more popular because you will win it and people will realize that you have been the victim who has been attacked rudely by Democrats and the media for more than two years.

Mr. President, your popularity has never dropped below 40 percent despite the repeated attacks against you, instead, it is going to rise above 60 percent because during the defense process you described all your achievements and the deceptions made by Democrats to Americans. The effective achievements are going to put you really at the door of re-election: Mexico's border wall will improve security; the economy is growing 2.1 percent in its GDP; unemployment is 3.6 percent, the lowest since 1969. Americans like you stop China from doing dirty trades and rob the country; that you make a better deal with Iran and Cuba and Americans see also with good eyes the good relationship with Israel, looking peace in the Middle East.

Mr. President, you know that you need to be impeached to save your future. Depending on the impeachment results, all investigations against you will be finished. From there, there will be no second investigation because the decision is taken by Congress which is the highest authority in the country. The impeachment won't proceed successfully because Americans do not like to accuse their presidents and see instability in the country: for example, Richard Nixon resigned from the presidency before being indicted to give calm; also congress didn't impeach the former president Bill Clinton, giving reassurance. So your presidential future will depend on Congress, Republicans, and Americans who want stability and continue seeing a non-traditional ruler.

NATIONALISM INSTEAD OF GLOBALIZATION

September 28, 2019

Mr. President, Albert Einstein said that nationalism is a childhood disease. It is the measles of mankind. I believe globalization was worse than measles and it is time to return to the mild disease of nationalism. In the last UN's General Assembly that you participated and even in the G7 summit you have insisted on nationalism and bilateralism instead of globalism. This suggestion has created confusion in people because they believe the world has returned to the xenophobia's blind hatred and blind passions that lead to wars. Nevertheless, you made an important differentiation between nationalism and patriotism that calmed people's spirits. Patriotism teaches us to adopt nationalism again without being blinded by hate but by everybody's responsibility and passion to make advance the country. The difference between old nationalism and the present nationalism is that in the latter everybody has the responsibility of developing his nation.

Although you may think globalism is an important system, may also believe the world wasn't still ready to assume globalism because has brought many problems. For example, when globalization came most countries did not have secured borders and neither effective immigration rules, creating a big mass of illegal immigrants who in some cases brought crimes in the form of terrorism, illegal drugs, human traffic, unauthorized arms business, and prostitution. Nationals weren't also ready to share the country's opportunities with foreigners, creating hate in the form of xenophobia. The culture was also affected because advanced countries appropriated other countries' cultures to have more productivity. Also, the power to rule freely was lost because the government is in the hands of international corporations.

It is well known that globalism integrated all the world including communist countries that wished to make business with capitalists. Communist countries took advantage of globalization to grow although they have continued to restrict freedom and to exploit people while their leaders are living in splendor. Mr. President, your idea about nationalism may help to understand clearly the difference between communism and capitalism currently. Communism has always applied nationalism through teaching to hate other countries' people; exploiting poor people without receiving incentives and denying people freedom. You offer nationalism for people to organize themselves, they can live freely and have what they want. Everyone in your nationalist country is free to do what he wants but applying freedom responsible to ensure his future and all the people around him.

YOU SLEEP WITH THE SNITCH

October 1, 2019

Mr. President, you know that betrayal often does not come from enemies but associates or friends. The most important now is to know who the whistleblower is because it is up to this to know if a serious crime of espionage was committed against you. A sophisticated spying system could have been configured to observe you. But also someone you know or who knows you could cooperate by delivering information. It could be possible that someone from any government office or the office of intelligence was spying on your campaign. About those possible sources you have to think about, and you could start by pointing out your closest associates.

These hypotheses can be true or false because what the whistleblower reported could be done with second-hand help, betraying you using a spy system. The nature of the information indicates that there may have been second-hand cooperation who could be present or have used an electronic spy system. The information revealed had a confidential rank and could only be shared with people of the same rank. But as the information was shared privately almost in the form of a whisper through a phone, it is possible the whistleblower was present when you talked about investigating the former vice president Joe Biden. So an electronic system connected to the phone could record the whispers, but the whistleblower could be also fed by people close to you who were there when you made the call phone.

The cell phone was made by you to Ukraine's president to ask him to investigate the former vice president Joe Biden and his son Hunter for corruption. You were sure the call was not being recorded because the information was hidden under a security system where is stored national security issues. However, someone close to you who was present that day described the call essence to the whistleblower. The whistleblower has said that you pressured Ukraine's president to deny economic aid to the country if he did not initiate an investigation of Biden. You said that you never pressured the president of Ukraine but the whistleblower affirmed you did.

Mr. President, you should find out that person who delivered information to the whistleblower because he betrayed the country. You could start thinking about those who you trust more like your lawyer, Mr. Giuliani, or Mr. Pompeo, the Secretary of State. They heard the call and knew about your plans. Think also about who of your close associates want to betray you and why. Mr. President, the most important is to understand that the conspirator betrayed you and the country too. You are interested Americans may know about the corruption developed during the Obama administration and all the dirt actions done to get you out of the presidency. I think Ukraine could be a good source to find the truth.

THE SNITCH WAS PLANNED

October 7, 2019

Mr. President, I think the truth is not for everyone but for those who have the courage to seek it. There is a question that Americans would like to know the answer and it is why did you say the words the whistleblower has revealed? Everything seems to have been planned to lead toward finding the corruption performed by the Obama administration, although it may cost you to be prosecuted for abuse of power. You are not afraid of being accused because there is not any crime on what the whistleblower has informed. Your words on the phone were absent of pressure and had the purpose of finding a truth that will benefit the country. So it is better to know how everything happened and why the whistleblower and his gang did that.

The whistleblower affirmed that through a phone call you pressured Ukraine's president to investigate the former vice president Joe Biden and his son for corruption; and to assure that action, you denied economic aid to Ukraine. The whistleblower also said you wanted to hide the phone call content in a secret system. However, that was not true because the phone call description was revealed totally. Besides, Ukraine's president has affirmed the phone called was made on good terms, he never received any pressure to investigate the former vice president, and Ukraine received the economic aid promised by the US.

This incident seems weird and Americans may believe you are crazy, but it is not. Beginning from Ukraine is a clever way of finding the truth about corruption in the Obama administration, In Ukraine, the former vice president Joe Biden and his son Hunter started the corruption with a corrupt Ukraine's oil company, then they continued the corruption in China. But this investigation is also going to lead to know how these countries and others helped Obama to conceive a plan for making you give up which developed into the idea of Russia conspiracy. Everything seems to be connected toward corruption and the wish to make you renounce by impeaching you.

Mr. President, you are uncovering the pot that contained the conspiracy that wanted to make you give up. It is times of overturning the coin and make the opposition pays all the offenses made against you. You were investigated for two years for conspiring with Russia to win the 2016 election; the investigation has continued because democrats want to impeach you, but they haven't found decided proves yet. Democrats have considered the phone call you made to Ukraine's president was an abuse of power and some consider you have to be impeached. However, the impeachment isn't going to progress because in advance you will show the truth where Obama and his team ruled for their benefit and not for the people.

TO THE KURDS AND OTHERS YOU'RE A TRAITOR

October 9, 2019

Mr. President, knowing your humble heart it is certain that you want the best for the country and the world too. However, you have been pointed by your allies the Kurds in the northeast of Syria as a traitor because they were left alone and defenseless after you ordered withdraw the troop and allowed Turkey's troops to enter the northeast of Syria. But you are not a traitor; your decision seeks to accomplish peace in the region. Everything seems contradictory but leaving the Kurds alone is a valuable strategy that allows those countries to solve their differences together without the presence of the US.

After destroying the Islamic State in the region of Syria with the help of Kurd fighters, you have believed that the soldiers should rest by returning to the country. You have also allowed the Turkey government to enter the northeast of Syria to solve the problems that the war has left. The government of Turkey needs to relocate Syria's people who invaded Turkey during the war. Also, Turkey has to solve its differences with the Kurds who live in Syria because they can start a war against Turkey, destabilizing the country. The Kurds are an ethnic group who are looking for a long time region to establish their country; that's why the Kurds became allies of the US so that it could provide military and political assistance.

In this war against the Islamic State, the Kurds have lost more than 10 thousand fighters, and wounded are the same amount. The Kurds have also Islamic State prisoners that no country wants to receive. Kurds' situation is difficult currently but more because they were left alone; that's why they need to find new allies to face the attack from the Turkey troop. This panorama could be the beginning of a new war because Turkey considered the Kurds its enemies, the Kurds can receive support from Iran, Syria, or Russia, and the Kurds are a big population disseminated for all the Middle East who wants to fight until they can get land to live in.

Mr. President, you know a new war represents a good business in weapons for the country, but I think you don't want another war in the Middle East, your wish to give peace to the region; you want also to protect the Kurdish population who have suffered terribly for almost one hundred years by trying to build the Kurdish state. Americans know that the Kurds are not going to be alone because you will be there to set the conditions for the Kurds won't be abused, to give asylum to those who need, to receive with respect the Islamic State prisoners and as a thank you to the Kurds, you will help them get the promised land.

FOX NEWS IS NOT YOUR ENEMY

October 11, 2019

Mr. President, the bad news and polls that lead to your defeat is what attracts the media and generates profits. Most of the polls have reflected negative numbers for you currently. Surveys show Democrats candidates leading polls and 50 percent of Americans want you to be impeached. This data makes you feel mad but much more when the negative numbers come from your ally, the Fox News channel. After observing the quantities, you said on Twitter that Fox News is not good in polls neither for the US. However, many people have refused your affirmation, considering Fox News is good at elaborating surveys, but many have also considered the numbers are not bad considering that you have received rude attacks from all over during more than two years.

The poll data that Fox News has shown may be true totally because it isn't easy to sustain a good image after being attacked by the media every day for three years. Besides, the numbers of the surveys cannot be different because you have faced a two years investigation and Democrats have continued censuring you. Besides, the poll numbers were almost the same as when the former president Bill Clinton faced impeachment in 1998 although Clinton wasn't attacked like you, he wasn't facing re-election and Clinton really lied to Americans.

It is not appropriate to affirm that Fox News is bad at doing surveys because that's not true. Fox News has been recognized as one of the best-doing polls. In the past, Fox News' polls were the best with a small margin of error. You have been right saying that Fox News was wrong in the 2016 poll when you won the presidency; however, Fox News's poll was right affirming Hillary Clinton would win the popular vote, and she won. Also, Fox News' survey was right saying Democrats would win the House of Representatives in the 2018 contest, and they won too. You could have said that about Fox News because you feel frustrated after seeing the negative data, but the media has to show its independence and quality.

Mr. President, I think you don't need to think too much about polls, instead, you need to think about how to be re-elected. Your goal has to be to win both the Electoral College and the popular vote. To win the election you need your party, Republican, near to you especially now when Democrats want to impeach you. The Republicans are going to support you in any plan and circumstance. Richard Nixon had to resign in 1974 because his party, the Republicans, denied his support; so think about how to join the party. Also, you have time to plan the campaign well because the Democrat candidate has not been selected yet. And you have advantages because currently, the power is in your hands. The most important is to gain the vote of Americans, the survey is not crucial, it is important that Americans may see that you work for them making America great again as you promised.

THERE IS ALWAYS POLITICAL INTERFERENCE

October 14, 2019

Mr. President, politicians act like saints because they always talk about the sins of others and never theirs. American politics has always been hypocritical. Previous administrations have sought foreign support to finance their campaigns and attack their opponents to win elections. Nobody had said anything about this alone until now that you are president. Democrats, Republicans, and the media were quiet. Now that Russia has been found to have interfered with the 2016 presidential election and that also you asked Ukraine's administration to investigate the former vice president Joe Biden and his son, everyone put the cry in the air. This a hypocritical behavior which means that this not a crime when traditional politics commit it, but it is a crime when you do. Mr. President, you have been the stone in the shoes of traditional politicians because you have never been a politician and you are uncovering corruption.

American laws have considered that foreign interference in elections or ask favors from a foreign country to influence political elections is a serious offense. That has to be so because otherwise personal interests are created and will affect the security and welfares of the country. For example, a foreign country may help a particular candidate to be the president because the country wants to have business preferences. A candidate may also ask a foreign country to help with network publicity to discredit his competitors. According to laws if that phenomenon happens, the winner should not be considered a legitimate president and has to be impeached.

Nevertheless, since the creation of the United States, no president has been impeached for using foreign interference but everyone commits that fault. Everyone is quiet about that because there is a traditional circle of politicians who covers the corruption. Mr. President, you uncovered this problem and for that, you are being investigated for conspiracy and abuse of power after asking Ukraine's president to investigate the former vice president Joe Biden for corruption. So far lawmakers have realized that the electoral system that prosecutes this problem does not work well and want to reform it immediately. Only until now when you are president lawmakers especially democrats have realized that the electoral system's commissioners are not named and so they never meet.

Mr. President, stopping foreign interference in a political campaign is very difficult because each country has its favorite candidate and will support its candidate. For example, North Korea, Israel, Russia, and Saudi Arabia are going to support you and will do anything for you to win. The same will do with other countries that will support other candidates, those countries don't need to ask the candidate if he needs help necessarily, they just help whoever best defend the interest of the country. Really it is very difficult to stop foreign interference. Currently, it is hard to order the world network to stop sending messages during the election time, no law prohibits that. What lawmakers can do is message Americans to motivate them for voting the best candidate; although, Americans already know that you are the best option to govern effectively and honestly.

WAR MUST BE A BUSINESS FOR THE UNITED STATES

October 17, 2019

Mr. President, you believe that war must be economically profitable or else there is no war. A political storm has arisen after you ordered to remove the troop from Syria. Democrats, some Republicans, and also some world leaders have criticized the departure of the troops, calling this a betrayal of the Kurds and also dangerous because the Islamic State fighters can reappear. No one only you have said that the withdrawal of the troop has economic reasons, and it is true; from the side that is looked at, everything has economic reasons. You have affirmed you don't want to fight a war that has a lot of costs instead you want to fight where you can get gains. Your words may mean that Syria is not important economically anymore and you want to locate the troops where you can get benefits. I think that is a good idea because whoever wants security must pay for it, and your ideas also suggest that you think of Americans first.

Syria's war that started in 2011 was a great gun business because it compromised many countries that fought for or against Syria's government. During the eight years of war, the US supported the Kurds to fight against Syria's government which meant a high economic cost. The troop withdrawal from Syria may mean now more gun business to other countries because the US leaves leaving another war on. The other war will be started by Turkey to annihilate the Kurds who are a threat. At the same time, other countries will support the Kurds and others the Turks. But since the war with Syria isn't over, there will always be an excuse to sell weapons.

However, the great gun business to the US comes now when you want to fight where can get good profits. That could mean that you want to make troops and military services a market that can be paid for by countries that need protection. That may be so because you ordered to place 2000 troops in Saudi Arabia where surely can get a lot of profit. Mr. President, I think the business may not be above moral values because your allies in Syria, the Kurds, are going to be killed by Turkey because you withdrew the troop, they are alone, and Syria's war doesn't represent a good profit. It is well known that you are loyal to your friends and want peace for the Middle East, so I believe you will ask Turkey's president to respect the life of the Kurds and everyone in the north of Syria.

REMOVE THE TROOP FROM SYRIA WAS PRUDENT

October 19, 2019

Mr. President, it seems that one of your strategies is to go back but to gain strength for the race. Republicans, some democrats, and world leaders have criticized the US's withdrawal troops from Syria. They have considered terrorism may rise again, the Kurds are defenseless at risk of being killed, Kurd's population may displace looking for protection, and a new war can arise if Turkey attacks the Kurds. Taking out the troop from Syria may be a mistake but could be a clever move too. The clever move was to allow Turkey's troops to occupy the north of Syria which will allow Turkey's government to organize all the problems that the war has left.

The troop withdrawal can be understood as a mistake because the troop leaves without making a peace agreement, leaves leaving an air of more war, leaves leaving Syria almost destroyed, civilians seeking refuge in other places, and the Kurds abandoned and in danger of dying. This environment is worse now than ten years ago when the war started. All the actors are enemies there currently: Syria, ISIS, Kurds, and Turkey. Syria may want to leave the Kurds out of northern Syria; Turkey may want to destroy the Kurds whom it considers his enemy, ISIS may want the Kurds to liberate their people to continue expanding their war, and the Kurds may want to fight for a land where they can build their country.

However, the departure of the troop and allow Turkey's troops to enter Syria may be a master play to organize the north without the presence of the US. Turkey's troops may force the Kurds to leave the north of Syria and go to Iraq where more Kurds are. So Turkey transfers its enemy from that border and Kurds may organize their community in Iraq. Turkey can also make Syrian people who moved to Turkey during the war to come back to Syria. Besides, Turkey can administrate the ISIS prisoners that the Kurds have. Mr. President, this plan shows that Turkey can play a better role there to solve problems and control the area well because it is its neighborhood. And it also shows that you are right, the troop doesn't need to be there and deserves to go back home which is thousands of kilometers away.

JUST FOR A CALL THEY WANT TO PROSECUTE YOU

October 23, 2019

Mr. President, there are many doubts about what you said in the phone call, but if there are doubts it is because you are on the right track to the truth. Democrats want to base the impeachment against you just from a phone call that you made to Ukraine's president asking him to investigate the Democrat candidate Joe Biden and his son for corruption. Can just a phone call be enough proof to accuse? The content of the phone call has to be irrefutable to decide if you deserve to be impeached, so the content needs to be supported by a credible source with credible content. So far the source seems to be credible because few people were present at the phone call and the content seems also credible because it is the reproduction of the phone call released by you. However, being present in the same place is not a guarantee of becoming a reliable source, and neither could be the transcription

The phone call was made on July 25 and several people were present there; one of them could be the whistleblower who informed about the phone's content. The whistleblower's identity has remained hidden but now it has emerged the coronel Alexander Vindman expert in Ukraine topics who was in the room when the phone call happened. Vindman has confirmed that you asked the president of Ukraine to investigate the former vice president Joe Biden. So far, no one has confirmed the coronel Vindman is the whistleblower but he seems to be. The coronel decided to denounce this to Congress because he has considered it inappropriate that the US president ask a foreign government to investigate a US candidate.

Mr. President, you have said there wasn't anything inappropriate about the conversation with the president of Ukraine that was made on good terms. The colonel Vindman for his part said that he heard something different, and this was that you pressured Ukraine's president to investigate the former vice president Joe Biden and his son for corruption. But answering the questions in the congress, Vindman has shown doubts about the real content of the conversation on the phone call. He said he believed that was the essence of the conversation. It is normal that there are doubts because the listener was far away from the speaker and you, Mr. President, speak fast; this makes it difficult to understand. Also, doubts may appear and increase after several days because people tend to forget details.

The only thing that could clarify the doubts was displaying the phone call transcription, and you did that. You made public the reproduction in writing, but the unknown whistleblower and colonel Vindman have affirmed it is incomplete. They said the part where you threaten Ukraine's president not to give money to the country is lost. It has been reported that you hid the missing part in a secret server because it contains confidential information. But hiding information is a regular activity that you can do because you have executive privileges to protect yourself and the country. I think it is important to hide that information because the cause of the threat is not clear; the president of Ukraine could be threatened with not providing resources because corruption in the country is great, or also if he does not investigate Biden for corruption.

Mr. President, with those inconsistencies in the information there is no need to worry; with that, any lawyer can defend you. The defender can ensure that the witnesses have doubts and the information is incomplete. The crime of which you are accused of abuse of power to force a foreign country to investigate a national candidate is not clear. It is time to lock all the information, so Democrats won't have any evidence and may refuse to start an impeachment process. But if Democrats want to accuse you of abuse of power, it is clear they don't care about the truth they just care about remove you and get the presidency.

FLORIDA IS NOW YOUR NEW RESIDENCE

November 5, 2019

Mr. President, I believe that the happiness of living somewhere is not in the luxuries of the house but the good soul of its inhabitants. The decision to move your residence to Florida was clever. Most people think about a place to live for retirement and they try to find many good reasons to choose that place. The reason to choose the place for retirement is generally the same for everybody: low tax income, safe place, good transportation system, friendly and educated people, nice weather and facilities for relaxing. Those are good reasons, but you think there are still many things to do before getting relaxed. One thing, for example, is to win the 2020 reelection and rule the country for four more years. Another thing is to solve your tax and financial problems that you have stored living a lifetime in New York. Mr. President, the state of Florida can provide you with conveniences to make a great political campaign, to manage your finances more accurately, and live retirement happily.

Most people may think you have changed the place of residence because you want to avoid taxes and also hide some tax evasion practiced when lived in New York. One reason for moving to Florida is indeed eluding taxation because you are paying high taxes in New York around 9 percent while in Florida there is no income or state taxation. So that was a good decision to protect your finances. But it isn't true that with the decision to move to Florida you wanted to hide tax evasion that you supposedly did while lived in New York. You know that it is impossible to avoid any investigation started in Manhattan; that will follow you wherever and will finish when everything is clear. So if you own something, everything will be known. Also, Florida isn't a fiscal paradise where people can go to hide their corruption; Florida is just a state that offers good things among those is the nice environment, and also there isn't property tax collection and no state tax for residents.

Florida is also a great state to win the reelection campaign. Policy experts have affirmed that whoever can win the vote in Florida will win the presidency. Mr. President, you expect to win the reelection by the Electoral College's highest number of votes and Florida provides 29, the highest number. Although you won Florida in the 2016 election, it is better to be living there to be sure of winning again. Many people from Latin America live in Florida and they may resent you because the immigration rules are tough right now. However, they will vote for you because they understand those measures organize and provide security to the country. In Florida, the financial support for the campaign won't be deficient either; that will be immense because, like you, many rich people made Florida their residence and they are going to vote and support you.

Mr. President, doing your residence in Florida was a good decision for your life and your family. Florida is a paradise everywhere with a nice community and beautiful weather. You are going to enjoy very much yourself with your family and the retirement life there. But in the meantime, the campaign is moving forward and you cannot forget your hometown, New York. New York is an important state to win the election because it gives also 29 Electoral College votes. To win NY's vote will be a challenge because you lost there in the 2016 campaign. I think you could win in New York because it is the main center of business where you developed your life and where many business people know you. New Yorkers appreciate that you are from there and have worked hard to develop the city greatly. You just have to remember people about that and that you love New York.

DEMOCRATS FINALLY DECIDED TO IMPEACH YOU

November 7, 2019

Mr. President, Democrats have decided to impeach you finally after voting positively to start the process. They have thought a lot about this but now they believe that there are enough arguments to accuse you. The arguments seem perfect to impeach you, but those can also be deliberated because there are irregularities. Democrats believe blindly that you abused the power by asking the president of Ukraine to investigate the former vice president Joe Biden and his son for corruption. They accepted a secret testimony from a whistleblower who affirmed that effectively you pressured Ukraine's president by denying economic aid authorized by Congress. All that information can be refuted because there are discrepancies, making this unbelievable; but democrats know the process is lost from the start.

The accounts are clear and Democrats know they will lose. They need 20 Republican votes in the Senate to complete the majority of 67. It is impossible to get that many votes because Republicans won't betray you, they want to continue in power, and so they will support you massively. Mr. President, you will win this fight and won't be removed, but Democrats will want to weaken you more to win the 2020 election. They are going to discredit you by collecting all the material that may describe well both the conspiracy with Russia to win the 2016 election and the abuse of power to ask a foreign country to investigate a national candidate. With this, they want to convince the Americans that you betrayed the country and the constitution.

The Democrats can succeed in discrediting you because they have a lot of power and most of the media support them. This week the Democrats showed their power by winning the government of Kentucky and especially Virginia where Republicans have governed for the last twenty years. This kind of failure is used by the media to talk badly about you, seeking to weaken you to make you lose points in the polls. For example, during the last past two weeks, the media discredited you greatly affirming you are a traitor of your allies because you withdrew the troop from Syria, allowed Turkey's troop entered to the north of Syria, leaving alone the US allies, the Kurds, to be killed by the Turks. However, betraying wasn't your plan, it was different but Democrats and the media showed this as if it had occurred.

Mr. President, Democrats are going to fail in their attempt to weaken you. At this moment, Nietzsche's sentence serves to say what will happen to you: "what doesn't kill makes it stronger". Democrats and the media have censured you brutally for three years and you have survived with favorable numbers in the polls. No president would have survived that fierce attack, but you did. Now the Democrats have spent most of the munition and have just a few bullets to use in the impeachment process that will begin next week. Instead, you have all the ammunition reserved. You can attack demonstrating that Democrats never accepted the 2016 defeat and from the first week of your administration they have tried dishonestly to remove you. You will also have the chance to describe all the corruption during the Obama administration and most importantly, you could show the greatest achievements during your administration.

HANG OUT WITH GOOD PEOPLE

November 10, 2019

Mr. President, what has happened in Virginia and Kentucky shows that good collaborators cost less than bad ones. The losses in Virginia and Kentucky are not an announcement about what will occur in the 2020 election. You are going to win the reelection with a large advantage over the Democrat candidate. However, those defeats teach that it is important to select the right candidate, the right person to rule the states, governors need to follow a remarkable plan to govern and they must govern for the people. For not complying with those principles, Virginia and Kentucky's people punished the Republicans by denying them reelection. Mr. President, Americans know you apply those postulates to rule but it is important to extend them to govern the states and in that way, there will be a great development in the country in general and the whole of the country will wear republican red.

For example, Matt Bevin wasn't really a good candidate to be reelected by Republicans in Kentucky. Bevin did a bad job during his administration that's why before elections, the polls gave him just 35 percent of favorability. During his government, Bevin did not grow anything to win the campaign. He attacked sharply an important field as is education trying to modify pensions and cutting resources. Also, Bevin's relationship with Republicans was distant, he didn't grow the party by creating a strong political base in Kentucky. In the end, Bevin lost by few votes but because you supported him making an important rally there, but he really lost because of him.

On the other hand, the failure in Virginia demonstrates that governors have to govern for the people through a precise plan. Republicans should know about this because they have been governed Virginia for almost a generation. They believed they would win again without paying for their mistakes. However, Virginia's people made Republicans pay for their mistakes relocating the power to Democrats. The Republicans' main mistake was that they didn't understand that currently Virginia's people including those from the suburbs are more educated people, multicultural and they demand more social services. For example, the people of Virginia considered it irresponsible that the use of weapons was not controlled after the attack in the Virginia Beach office where a man killed 12 people.

Mr. President, you are doing a great job and this has to be extended throughout the country. The US map has to be republican red and to achieve this the governors must work hard as you do. The failure in Virginia and Kentucky should not repeat and neither occurs in other states. To assure these, you must monitor the work of the governors; you cannot run a political campaign accompanied by bad candidates. If the Republican rulers of the states may solve people's necessities, they are responsible and work hard to unify the party, the Republican Party will govern forever.

THE IMPEACHMENT WILL HAVE THE OPPOSITE RESULT

November 15, 2019

Mr. President, the only people you should believe in now is your enemies because you know what they want. Democrats started the impeachment inquiry against you for abuse of power after you asked the government of Ukraine to investigate for corruption the former vice president Joe Biden and his son. Votes in the Democratic House were partisan: the votes were divided between the two parties and in the end, the democratic vote won and with it the decision to prosecute you. The House will start now to plan the impeachment process and its rules. The decision to impeach you wasn't easy to make because the democrats wanted to be sure of winning. They wanted to be sure about the essence of the crime and the support of the Americans. However, Democrats voted this without knowing the essence of the crime, when the polls are divided and all Republicans support you.

For these reasons, the impeachment will be a total failure and will only be essence for the press. Understanding the reason why the Americans divided their thoughts in the polls it is possible to understand why the accusation will be a failure. Fifty percent of Americans are with you because they understand the investigation has been just political persecution against you. The Democrats never accepted the 2016 defeat and they planned to discredit you, accuse, and look for other ways to make you abdicate.

Democrats have followed the plan rigorously to make you resign from the first day of your presidency, launching a two years investigation against you for conspiring with Russia to win the 2016 election. The result of the two years of the investigation did not like the Democrats because you were acquitted, so the House started a parallel investigation. The Democrats soon understood that this new investigation against you has also no future and they started to feel hopeless. The optimism arose again when a whistleblower announced that you abused power because you asked the president of Ukraine through a phone call to investigate for corruption the former vice president Joe Biden and his son. Without reflecting very much about the matter, the House of Democrats announced that you have committed a grave crime asking a foreign government to investigate a national candidate.

This new accusation will be another failure because no one knows who the whistleblower is and the sources that have accused you are not first-hand; they heard about it from other people. Those continuous attacks during almost three years make you a victim who deserves consideration and respect. Americans understand that and also understand that you have made a good job as president improving the economy, employment and security. Republicans know also that you have done good work and they will support you. This impeachment process tends to be a total failure for Democrats and a great success for you. Mr. President, the impeachment will give you more popularity, that's why more Americans will be with you giving their vote to reelect you.

YOU WANTED TO BE IMPEACHED

November 17, 2019

Mr. President, with this process of accusation you are risking a lot but nothing is achieved if you are not in danger. The impeachment process against you started formally and some witnesses will testify in the House of Representatives. You are accused mainly of three offenses: abuse of power, bribery, and conspiracy. According to the nature of the sources and the information collected, it seems you committed those transgressions. Who witnessed the transgressions has said that you tried to bribe the president of Ukraine by denying his country economic aids authorized by the US Congress if he didn't open an investigation for corruption against the former vice president Joe Biden and his son. That indication is considered a plot against a Democratic candidate who is running for the 2020 election. That suggestion is also viewed as an abuse of power because you are applying your position as president to affect an opponent and so win the next elections.

Many Americans may affirm that you didn't need to bribe someone to try to win the next election because you can win without doing that. That's true, you have governed well improving the economy, employment, salaries, and security. Also, all Republicans support you, and most importantly, the Americans who voted for you in the last campaign are still with you. You didn't really need to do that but you did; so what you did needs to have another explanation. There are two explanations about that: one, you wished badly to be accused to get more people's attention and popularity. Two, you wanted to use the impeachment process to give to know the corruption practiced during the Obama administration.

Mr. President, it seems that you yourself took the risk of being impeached because you knew beforehand that you would not be prosecuted. Therefore, you took advantage of that knowledge to do both: to be more popular and to let know about the corruption practiced during the Obama administration. That doesn't seem like a correct way to do that but Americans will appreciate your courage. Ukraine was a center of corruption, and Biden and his son Hunter took this country to operate. Because of that, you asked the current president of Ukraine to investigate the conspiracy of the Democrats to make you give up as a 2016 candidate and as president too. And also, you asked him to let know why Biden's son worked in an oil company of Ukraine investigated for corruption, earning an extremely high salary.

Corruption during the Obama administration has no limits, but that corruption was the worst because it was by omission. Omission because he did nothing special although he was called the black president of hope. The country did not progress much because Obama acted poorly. Obama dedicated himself to cultivating a bureaucratic group and forgot the progress of the country. There is nothing extraordinary to show from Obama even though Americans expected that Obama could unite the society more and end racism, but that did not happen. Instead, the rate of violence was high, racism and social discrimination never disappeared. Mr. President, nobody was aware of Obama's corruption because among the politicians they hide everything. Fortunately, you are not a politician, so you are not hypocritical to silence evil and have denounced that regular politicians have cheated the country forever.

THE IMPEACHMENT SEEMS TO BE A COUP D'ÉTAT

November 20, 2019

Mr. President, everything that has happened so far and how it has been worked indicates that the Democrats are conspiratorial experts. There are reasons to believe the impeachment is a coup d'état that Democrats want to give you. The pieces of evidence have shown that it is a coup against you and the people who named you as president. Democrats have made all kinds of bad actions during the last three years to get you out of the presidency. They put most of the media against you, informing everyday bad and fake news about your government. The Democrat House wants to present you as a criminal after ordering several investigations. Also, they don't want to let you rule by blocking all your projects. As they haven't achieved anything, the House ordered to start a formal investigation to weak you and so try to win the next election.

The coup d'état has developed in two parts: one started three years ago after you took the White House and its purpose was to make you renounce through attacking you every day with fake news. As this coup failed, the second part began with the announcement of a political trial which had the purpose of putting you in jail. Everything seemed like a nightmare: just one week after you took the presidency, the media started to talk about you, your family, and your businesses badly. The media declared you as mentally unable to handle the country after you ordered shut down the government if Congress didn't approve resources to build the border wall with Mexico. The worst nightmare came soon when Congress ordered an investigation of you for conspiring with Russia to win the 2016 election.

Russia's investigation was developed by a special counsel, Robert Mueller, who had all the power to inquiry anyone and all resources to achieve this successfully. Muller spent two years and almost 40 million trying to discover how you colluded with Russia to win the election. Every day the media through its guests affirmed that you, your family, and your friends conspired with Russia. This kind of persecution has never been seen before against a president and it was difficult to survive it. However, you resisted and Muller could never find conclusive pieces of evidence.

Everything seems like the attacks would stop there but Democrats did not give up to make you quit. The Democrat House ordered a parallel investigation to that of Muller, subpoenaing many of your assistants. In the end, the House felt disappointed because it also found no evidence but suddenly another intrigue appear against you.

This intrigue gave the Democrats serious motives to order an accusation against you. Democrats found then three alleged crimes committed by you: abuse of power, conspiracy, and bribery. Supposedly you used the political power to bribe the president of Ukraine to investigate former vice president Joe Biden and his son for corruption. This action was considered a conspiracy accomplished against Biden who like you is running for the presidency. Democrats knew the accusation against you won't be successful because they didn't have in the senate enough votes but anyway, launched the inquiry because they want to weak you before elections. Mr. President, all those events show that it was a coup d'état but you were victorious; now the Americans will reward you by electing you president again.

POLITICS NOW MEANS HAVING AND KEEPING POWER

November 24, 2019

Mr. President, what's in the Democrats is an exaggerated ambition for power. The second week of declarations in the House of Representatives has finished, teaching there that nothing is more important than getting power. To prove that affirmation it is enough to reproduce the words of Mr. Schiff, the Democratic committee chairman: "All Congress impeached Nixon in 1974 but now the problem to impeach is Congress". Of course, congress is different now than it was in Nixon's time. In Nixon's time, everybody believed in the constitution, laws, and decisions were bipartisan but now everybody wants to have power breaking the laws. Currently, there is a bipartisan war to hold the power and no one and nothing cares about the principles written in the constitution. In today's session, everyone accused each other rudely and also defended themselves aggressively, but no witnesses had solid truths.

Every day's constant has been the dishonest attack among parties to get power. Democrats nourished that dishonest constant for the last three years because they never accepted you had won the presidency. For them, it was unacceptable to have lost to a person with no political experience and to be ruled by him. Democrats attacked first aggressively to make you quit. They affirmed you won the 2016 election with tricks conspiring with Russia and they ordered an investigation. The investigation lasted two years but they found nothing conclusive; however, Democrats continued confronting you. Mr. President, you counterattacked saying the democrats have conspired to spy on your campaign, and also this investigation has been a coup Democrats wanted to give you.

The impeachment was the continuation of a war that has lasted for three years; in that war, you have defended yourself intelligently and have attacked without rules. Republicans and some media support you. Democrats fight claiming that you bribed the president of Ukraine denying economic aid if he didn't investigate the former vice president Joe Biden and his son for corruption. Democrats considered the bribe action was a conspiracy against Biden because he is a campaign candidate currently. Republicans defended you saying that that wasn't bribery or conspiracy that instead you were protecting the country from corrupt people. Republicans asked the House of

Representatives to order Biden and his son Hunter that they appear as witnesses to testify. But the House denied that petition saying that the inquiry is about what the president has done.

At the witness presentation session at the House of Representatives, the Democrats believed the witnesses would give strong evidence but it wasn't like that. The evidence was second-hand heard by other people; the evidence was also about personal feelings and opinions. Republicans used that weakness to ask witnesses directly if they had seen the president committed any crime, and their answers were negative; so the session was like a circus with nothing serious. Then the media that are with the Democrats began to play dirty editing the testimonies, displaying just fragments where they speak about you badly. Also, the media directed the audience to say what they wanted to hear.

Who will win this fight? For the moment, the impeachment process will be won by you because the Senate will take the last decision by voting and Republicans are the majority there. The fight for the presidency will be tough because Democrats and the media will continue to attack by discrediting you. But there are strong reasons to believe you will be reelected. One, Americans are tired of the traditional politicians who have been working for them and not for the people. You made Americans known about politicians' selfishness that compared to you who is not a politician you have done more than them. Second, you have made a good job as president. The country's economy is successful, employment record is high and unemployment is low; security has also improved after announcing the construction of the border wall with Mexico and placing troops there. Finally, none of your opponents show the fiber, vitality, and character that you have.

BLOOMBERG IS REALLY A DANGEROUS ENEMY

November 29, 2019

Mr. President, don't worry about the wealth of Bloomberg worry about gaining followers. The former New York's mayor, the billionaire Mr. Michael Bloomberg, joined the campaign for the presidency, and many people would have wondered why he did that if he has no chance of winning. Bloomberg had impressive achievements as mayor of New York for three periods but that record doesn't help because he joined the program too late. He would love to be president of the US, but Bloomberg is too old, 77, and Americans consider age carefully before voting. Also, currently, most Americans didn't know anything about Blomberg's political ideas because he hasn't run the political campaign, sharing the stage with other candidates, and answering the media questionnaire. Besides, Bloomberg doesn't meet the campaign requirements because he has not enough donors and polls putting him below the fourth percent.

What seems to be Bloomberg's plan if he knows he will lose? Bloomberg's plan is the same as the Democrats which is to make you lose votes. Bloomberg may resent you because you left New York to move to Florida, after all, New York has the most expensive tax rate, you said. That is true, New York is expensive in terms of taxes and almost in everything; maybe many New Yorkers hate Bloomberg because he raised New York's tax rate. Probably Bloomberg hates the bad image you gave about him and the city. With his fortune, Bloomberg can do many things to achieve his plan: he can move voters toward the Democrats' side by buying consciences. Bloomberg can also buy expensive publicity to promote the democrat candidate Joe Biden.

Mr. President, Bloomberg's plan may mean there will be a fraud and you should be very vigilant. You should advise in time to the electoral committee about any suspicious purchase of votes or people who vote fraudulently. Also, you have to watch the vote count carefully because vote juries can change them. Americans know you won't cheat in the elections because you have demonstrated been an honest person. To win the reelection you just need to work for the country hard and honestly every day; that kind of work will be your best publicity which costs zero pesos and it is different than Bloomberg's plans.

YOU CAN'T BE A WITNESS

December 3, 2019

Mr. President, you don't have to play the Democrats' game because everyone cheats. Nancy Pelosi, the House of Representative chairman, and all Democrats have invited you to go next week to the House to give testimony on the subject that is accused. They want you to be at the same time witness and accused of abuse of power and bribery, crimes that you supposedly committed. In other words, Democrats are inviting you to kill yourself politically. They want to sit you in that court that still don't have precise proofs, that haven't given you a fair process, where its committee has the obligation to develop the investigation and give it to the Senate, but it has not concluded. Democrats definitely want to sit you there to humiliate you by asking all kinds of rude questions. Mr. President, you don't need to go to that funeral because that is not yet your death.

Mr. President, you don't need to attend that invitation because that will be a political loss for you. The House of Representatives started an accusation process against you because you apparently forced the government of Ukraine to investigate for corruption the former vice president Joe Biden and his son Hunter. The information about this was given by a whistleblower whose identity is unknown. The House's sessions have been two weeks of hearings witnesses, but everything has been unfair and a failure. The House didn't allow you to present your witnesses or publicly give the whistleblower identity who secretly accused you. After two weeks of hearings, the House lawmakers haven't been able to prove that you bribed the Ukraine president to investigate Biden. If Democrats still don't have a conclusive investigation they cannot invite you to testify; therefore, they cannot send the impeachment to the Senate and should close the case. Anyway, you have executive privileges to decline the invitation.

Nevertheless, the democratic representatives have to vote a resolution accusing you of abuse of power if they want the Senate to judge you. Without strong evidence, the House will vote the resolution which it will win because the majority of democrats want to destroy you. The story in the Senate will be different because Republicans are a majority there and they will support you immensely. Mr. President, as you know well, the whole process ends in the Senate and you will be acquitted. The process is like that, the Senate is your natural judge and it will give the last word that everybody must obey; so previous presidents have acted when they were investigated. The Senate will do what the House didn't do which was to make a fair process calling the witnesses of both parties, providing solid evidence, and speaking without political interest. Although this accusation is against you and not against Biden, the Senate, in the end, could clarify Biden's abuse of power and Hunter's corruption, so Americans are going to understand how the previous administration acted wrongly.

SING THE TRUTH ABOUT NATO

December 5, 2019

Mr. President, everyone needs security and the best gift to building a peaceful future is supporting security in the present. You have taken hard tasks that former presidents avoided and one was to tell openly the members of the NATO that they are not adding enough money to the organization. Maybe previous administrations avoided giving that message because they wanted to keep NATO's unity and friendship. However, NATO's unity seems to be broken and that has caused problems inside the organization. The chaos within the organization was unveiled this week on NATO's 70 anniversary. Macron, the French president, started saying NATO is brain dead; then some members made fun of you after you asked for more money. The president of Turkey put conditions to continue in the organization, and you left the meeting suddenly and came back to Washington. Mr. President, thanks to your courage to speak and ask for more resources, it seems the time has come to reorganize NATO.

For many, reorganizing NATO could be easier than creating another organization. NATO was created in 1949 after the Second War to face the expansion of communism. Communism continues alive and other dangers have added currently as the great power of China, the expansion of the Islamic State, Russia's wishes over Baltic territories, Iran and North Korea is a nuclear menace, Israel and Palestine are always in a cold war. Also, Turkey wants NATO to consider the Kurds as a terrorist group. All those risks are near and around Europe; Europe cannot face it alone because is weak militarily, so Europe needs to continue depending on NATO's military support and will have to attend to your request about money.

In the summit, some of the leaders showed that they are not interested in the organization, but they need to think that building a new military organization to defend Europe is expensive. You see that the problem is that countries do not want to spend money on their security, that's why they mock and speak badly of NATO. For example, Emmanuel Macron, the president of France, said NATO has brain dead but without giving further explanations. Erdogan, the president of Turkey, wants NATO to solve an internal problem of his country such as the war with Kurds.

Mr. President, you don't see NATO with brain dead; the problem you see is lack of money and organization. You consider Europe has to pay more money for its security because the greatest dangers are all around there. The US is the country that gives more money to NATO, around 3 percent of its GDP, although the US has the most powerful military force around the world. I think countries have to pay for their security and you want them to do that. You can offer the US military power to face quickly and effectively any risk in Europe. And as you are a business person, you have considered that security is much more expensive than what has been paid so far. To face this problem means to win enemies, but you don't care about that; you just think about the interests of the country that previous presidents did not.

AMERICANS VOTE FOR THE PRESIDENT'S FAMILY TOO

December 9, 2019

Mr. President, the bond that unites the family is not in money or genes, but in the respect and joy, they share. The media has affirmed that there is a rivalry between your wife, Melania, and your daughter, Ivanka, who seems to want to play the role of the first lady. This news may be another fake news from the media that tries to create a bad atmosphere in your family. Melania and Ivanka complement each other well and both help you to achieve the administration effectively. People have seen Ivanka on some occasions playing the role of the first lady probably when Melania is attending other tasks. For example, Ivanka took that role when Melania was outside visiting other countries. That should be so to make everything more functional. But if there is a rivalry between the two, you have to stop it for the benefit of the family, the administration, and the next campaign.

It is well known that the president's daughter can be the first lady if the president's wife died or they are divorced. However, Americans prefer a wife as the first lady to a daughter, they do not approve of rivalry in that role; for them, the president's wife is the first lady and that is so. Rivalry for the role of the first lady would be a disaster for your reelection because that shows that the president's family is disintegrated and has no principles. Americans could see that problem worse than the conflict with North Korea and it could reduce your credibility greatly.

Everybody wants to see in the president's family a model of respect that represents the country well. The president's family must be integrated, respectful, educated, and compassionate. Those values cannot be pretended, cannot be false, and cannot be something that is not because people identify falsehood. Americans are going to vote for a president but also for the president's family who must hold human principles. If there is a war in the family for power, people won't vote for you and will remove your support. Mr. President, you have to work every day to build a generous family who avoids retaliation, hate, and instead love, and likes to serve selflessly.

THE AMERICAN DREAM FOR REFUGEES

December 10, 2019

Mr. President, the best way the United States can find itself is by diving into refugee and immigrant care. North Dakota has voted to accept a quota of refugees, contradicting your order not to accept refugees in the country. To make this decision was hard for North Dakota's people but in the end, their generosity prevailed by voting 2-3 for taking this measure. Both you and the state of Dakota have spoken about this matter and agreed on this but later, the vote showed that people preferred to be hospitable as they had always been.

Your idea of stopping the entry of refugees into the country is based on important arguments. One argument is wanting to make America great again which was stopped a long time ago. Your idea of making America great again is important because other countries like China are improving faster and better because they are thinking about themselves. You want to organize and make strong the house which is a great challenge. All Americans in the US deserve to have work before any foreigner; also business has to be the best as well as its internal production, infrastructure, communication, and internal security. All those challenges are good arguments to deny the entry of refugees into the country.

However, North Dakota's people believe that it is important and necessary to accept refugees because America was founded on principles of generosity and hospitality. Denying support to anyone is not Americans natural procedure, people of North Dakota said. But they also think about refugees because they need a cheap labor force to work the land. North Dakota's people consider the economy is going through a great moment and they need a lot of people to work there. Someone said there: it was funny to be voting for just a quota of 25 refugees if what they need are at least 25 thousand refugees who can work on many jobs.

Mr. President, the quota of refugees the US is accepting currently is very insignificant and it shouldn't be like that because what the US is today is due to the work of foreign labor. People from all over the world who were in wars or suffering starvation were accepted generously by the US but they didn't come to do anything, they came to help to build and develop the country. The US must be always thankful for the foreign labor force and he should never turn his back on them. You could also achieve the idea of making America great again accepting foreigners who can work in fields where there is a lack of labor force. It is important to realize that exporting people is vital to develop the country. Mr. President, you can make wide the immigrant policy and it will be helpful for everybody and everyone will be grateful to you.

DO NOT FIGHT WITH CHILDREN

December 16, 2019

Mr. President, I believe children are being used all over the world to manipulate humanity on issues that adults cannot or do not want to solve. The message you sent to Greta Thunberg, the 16 years old environment activist, created controversy but that seemed like you wanted to give her a bit of good advice. You said that it is better she could take care of her health well, has fun with a friend watching a movie, and can be relaxed. Your message that was qualified as sarcasm by the media created a big disagreement among the population, especially the young. Mr. President, you should avoid that kind of controversy, especially with children because people are very sensitive about issues assumed by young people. This debate with Greta was used by your opponents to attack you rudely, showing you as an enemy of the young, of the climatic effects, and it gave a lot of importance to her that she is now considered a heroine.

Greta has been compared absurdly with the French heroine Joan of Arc who was burned at the stake for heresy and for leading the French army against the British. The Time Magazine also named Greta the person of the year 2019 because has sent a few messages denouncing climate change and asking to control the carbonic gas emissions. Time Magazine knows that other people more than Greta deserve the honor of being the year's person, as Hong Kong's leaders who have been fighting for democracy for many years. This support from the media plus that of important people like the former Democrat candidate Hillary Clinton and the former first lady Michelle Obama have made Greta Thunberg very popular, reaching more than 4 million followers.

Greta Thunberg's activism has been just emotional without rational arguments and it talks about the same environmental problem that everyone knows. Currently, the environmental problem should be a shame for all world leaders because they haven't solved this problem after spending a long time. Anyway, this problem cannot be solved emotionally as Greta wants to do; it has to be solved objectively. For example, she traveled by ship from Europe to New York for 20 days to teach that traveling by plane is the most polluting. Everybody knows that is better to be in New York in eight hours than in twenty days, but no one contradicted her nor the media because the purpose was to attack you.

Mr. President, Greta Thunberg's show is not to save the world from carbon dioxide it is to make you very unpopular, that people hate you and make you fall in the polls. The media has involved your family in this problem by asking your wife Melania to talk about your mockery of Greta, as she defends children from bullying. The same thing that she has done defending her son Barron, 13 years old so that strangers do not involve him in politics. Also, the media mix Greta's environmental activism and her sickness, Asperger, to make you look like a monster attacking a sick young person who is working hard to save the world from warming. Definitely, Greta's Thunberg image could affect your picture; therefore, it is better to let her do her environmental campaign without referring to it.

THE IMPEACHMENT PROCESS WILL BE A CIRCUS

December 19, 2019

Mr. President, any way you look at it the impeachment against you will be detrimental for the justice, parties, and the country. The vote that will be placed this week in the House of Representatives to prosecute you will be like a game: above all things, the Democrats have decided to impeach you; and Republicans, above all things too, have decided to refuse the impeachment. Democrats haven't respected the due process, the truth, and the law; and Republicans want to do the same when the process goes to the Senate. In the end, the division between the parties will be significant, respect for justice will be minimal, and Americans will feel that there is no governing structure.

This negative effect is because Democrats did not accept the 2016 election defeat and they started to fabricate an accusation on you. This false impeachment is similar to former President Andrew Johnson's process which was an act of revenge because in 1867 Johnson fired an official without the consent of Congress. But it is different than former President Bill Clinton's accusation in 1998 because he committed a proven crime and lied under oath. So far, the House of Representatives has failed to prove that you committed a crime despite taking three years of investigation and hearing many witnesses. However in the end without a solid case, the House decided to impeach you, demonstrating it is an act of revenge like what happened to former President Andrew Johnson.

Everybody knows the House will vote positively to impeach you this week and it is possible to visualize the fight between Democrats and Republicans when the Senate receives the House's impeachment confirmation. Democrats are going to defend the impeachment decision with all their weapons and Republicans are going to justify the absolution with everything too. However, as the Democrats know you will be exonerated because Republicans are a majority in Senate, they want to leave the idea to the Americans that you are an illegitimate president who abused power and obstructed justice. In the meantime, Americans will understand that there is no justice in the country, also there aren't ethical principles, and politics is a spectacle made by politicians to deceit people.

DEMOCRATS WANT TO INFLUENCE THE PROCESS

December 24, 2019

Mr. President, in this investigation against you both parties have broken the law: there has been constant persecution, there has been no due process, and important proves have been hidden, and some aides have committed crimes. Having this corrupt environment, the House of Representatives ended the investigation approving by the majority of votes to impeach you and by issuing the resolution formally accusing you. According to the Constitution, the House's decision has to be submitted to the Senate where will start a hearing and it will decide by voting if you must be removed as president. However, the trial hasn't started yet and it is already marked by corruption because the House has decided not to send yet the resolution to, trying to manipulate the Senate process.

Democrats have wished intensely to remove you from office and now that the House's resolution has been held by the lawmakers it is because they are planning something morbid. The Speaker of the House, Nancy Pelosi, knows there is nothing to do and there is no time to plan something wrong because the resolution must be sent to the Senate as required by the constitution. The House's examination has already finished and now the Senate has to start its examination too to decide finally if you should be removed from office. Democrats know there are a majority of Republican senators in the Senate and they will all vote in your favor to keep you in office. Nancy Pelosi said that she would withhold the declaration of impeachment until she is sure the Senate will hold a fair trial.

The idea of withholding the impeachment articles by the House of Representatives seems to be a plot to seek Republican support in the Senate vote. Democrats need at least twenty Republicans who want to vote against you, but that's impossible to get. So the plot goes toward showing you as a criminal, adding more crimes to the investigation, and use the Senate stage to discredit you by reviving the Russia investigation that accused you of a conspirator. Pelosi tries to gain time to see if a star witness appears and he can reveal the whole truth, or some more Republicans want to join to betray you, so saving the circus set up so far by the Democrats.

Mr. President, what you have to do is to accelerate the trial in the Senate to avoid intrigues and manipulation. To do that, you can find support in the Supreme Court that can order the House of Representatives to apply the Constitution by sending the resolution of indictment to the Senate, and the Senate can follow the trial that must be decided by vote. According to constitutional experts, the House of Representatives ended its trial and the Senate now must lead its judgment by announcing the process rules, applying those until a decision is taken by vote. The trial has to be formal but uncomplicated: the House communicates its accusatory arguments, your lawyers are heard there defending you and in the end, Senators will vote. The Senate's trial is as simple as that;

it isn't another long investigation as Democrats want to impose. The essence of this trial is to decide by vote if you leave or remain as president.

YOU ARE BETTER THAN JOE BIDEN

January 2, 2020

Mr. President, you can disarm your political opponent Joe Biden by showing his negligence for forty years as a politician. There is the belief that you got yourself prosecuted to publicize yourself and the reelection campaign. That could be so although sounds estrange and immoral it could be valid action if it had the noble purpose of uncovering corruption. The House of Representatives voted to impeach you for abuse of power and obstruction of justice after you asked the government of Ukraine to investigate for corruption your political contender the former vice president Joe Biden and his son Hunter. Now everybody knows you are impeached, also that there was corruption during the Obama administration, and also you are more popular. But I think you didn't need to seek prosecution to show Biden's corruption and weaknesses because Americans know that. Biden is old, has not a good health record and he has always been an incongruous politician.

Mr. President, you have called Biden the 'sleepy Biden' because of the lack of intensity in his speaking and lack of energy in the body too. You have considered Biden at his age and poor spirit cannot face the many and tough country's problems. Current Biden's age, 77, is a problem because hardly he could complete one period at the presidency, understanding he had suffered from brain cancer and this health problem could affect his government. Biden's lack of spirit comes from a sad story that continues influencing his life. Biden lost his wife and daughter in a car accident and later his son Beau died of brain cancer. Hunter, Biden's son, is another sad story because he has consumed illicit drugs, alcohol and he is been investigated for corruption and laundering money after he made business with a corrupt company of Ukraine and with some Chinese corporations.

Since Joe Biden was discovered plagiarizing in college, it projected that Biden would never act correctly. Maybe Biden chose politics as a form of life because he realized there he could act wrongly, get forgiveness and be rich and famous. Joe Biden became rich and famous working in politics for almost forty years but his background shows that he always joined to the wrong sides. Biden supported cutting welfare increasing people's poverty; He also accepted racism avoiding school integration with black people and supporting massive incarceration to keep black people in jail. He also supported the war with Iraq. In general, most of Biden's career is marked by the style of letting go, letting time pass, by attacking minorities, and by enjoying the honey of politics because there are few achievements to show on more than thirty years as a lawmaker and eight as vice president.

Mr. President, Joe Biden arrived at the 2020 election without having a clear idea about what kind of politician he is. He said his ideas come from right and center but he has always acted as conservative. It seems it has been difficult for Biden to adjust the past with the present which demands more knowledge, justice, and freedom. That lack of knowledge makes Biden makes gaffes frequently, he cannot respond to the media questionnaires appropriately and don't have a clear plan to govern. During his role as Vice President, Biden build a strong circle of bureaucrats to keep power forever but you, Mr. President, broke that circle after you won the presidency.

Thanks to your work as president, Americans could know the corrupt form as politicians have made politic, hiding corruption themselves, letting go, and getting past the time while the country goes back wrongly.

WITHOUT QASSEM SOLEIMANI THE WORLD IS SAFER

January 7, 2020

Mr. President, Soleimani's death shows the laxity and negligence of the past administrations building the path of death for many soldiers. The Iranian general Qassem Soleimani was killed at a military operation ordered by you and this raised the question if you had acted correctly under the protocol of international laws. Answering this has been difficult because international laws may generate controversy. But under the unilateral rule that the US can attack to defend their militaries and the country, you acted correctly. So the US acted in self-defense because Soleimani led a criminal group dedicated to killing American soldiers in the Middle East. But if this rule looks for protecting soldiers abroad, this makes no sense that the previous administration had not acted promptly to kill Soleimani. Unfortunately, Bush and Obama didn't do anything to stop Soleimani and the consequence was sad because Soleimani's terrorist group killed hundreds of American soldiers and civilians.

Former President Bush and Obama have said they acted correctly because they wanted to avoid a war with Iran and they also acted prudently because no one knew how Soleimani planned to act. The point is hundreds of American families mourns their relatives who were killed by Soleimani and you, Mr. President, was the only president who did justice to this. You acted under the figure contemplated in the domestic Constitution, Article II, and UN's Security Council about self-defense to prevent future attacks. The self-defense figure allows a country to respond immediately to an attack although a preventive action may create controversies because it means to attack to prevent an attack that may happen or not.

In this case, soldiers needed always to be ready because attacks were imminent at any time. Everyone knew well for years that Soleimani moved around the region freely planning new forms to attack the troops. Soleimani attacked generally placing explosives on the road to blow up troop caravans. Lately, he had used drones to attack ships carrying oil killing civilians, and it was also believed that drones would be used to attack the troops. Before Soleimani was killed there were signs that Soleimani was going to attack again. At that moment, there was a violent protest in front of the American embassy in Iraq and an American civilian has been killed. The protest was more violent every moment, terrorists infiltrated it, and Soleimani had planned the protest to continue with more attacks.

The world is really safer without the monster of Soleimani, as you said; and Iran surely will think twice before attacking. Those who acted incorrectly were the former president Bush and Obama who were tolerant of terrorism allowing Soleimani to organize calmly attacks that ended the life of hundreds of soldiers. Their excuse was that they wanted to avoid a war it is not a valid excuse because the US has all the military power to intimidate any enemy effectively. They also said that was a lack of information but again, it isn't a valid excuse because there was accurate information from a long time ago about Soleimani. So. Bush and Obama should face a trial for omission and negligence to attack the enemy and for the death of militaries.

AFTER SOLEIMANI DEATH, IRAN WILL KNOW THAT YOU DON'T PLAY

January 10, 2020

Mr. President, past administrations failed to neutralize Soleimani because they were bureaucracies that only wanted to save their prestige. After you ordered General Qassem Soleimani to be killed, people eagerly expected Iran's revenge and finally, it developed this Wednesday. Ten missiles were dropped on two military bases in Iraq where coalition soldiers were stationed. The attack was confirmed by Iran's government, by the US military agencies, and you confirmed there weren't casualties. This attack can be symbolic because Iran may want to send a message that can be understood as war or negotiation. On the one hand, Iran may be saying that he is a strong enemy because he knows how to handle powerful weapons; on the other, Iran may be looking for a negotiation.

The attack is really significant because it was used arms of short-range with great precision that can arm on its fly. Some of the missiles hit the exact target as if it had entered through a buttonhole. The missiles that hit the target well, destroyed empty facilities and respected facilities where soldiers were camping. This action scares everyone because it seems Iran knows everything about the Coalition and the US's military organization there. After all, the missile shot just over the facility where there was no personal. Probably Iran's agency intelligence knows more about the Coalition troops stationed in Iraq than the Coalition itself. And it was also scary to see the images about the destruction of Iraq's military location by the missiles of Iran.

This attack can also be giving a conciliatory message. Respecting the life of the American troops may be Iran's sign to negotiate; Iran may be warning that everybody is at risk of dying if there is no negotiation. The missing missile that did not hit the target could be another Iran's sign for dialogue. Mr. President, respecting the life of the troop is a good sign for you to seek to negotiate with Iran. I think this moment is the right time to negotiate with Iran's regime because the majority of Iranians want freedom, justice, democracy and they are against the government after it unintentionally targeted a commercial airplane killing 176 passengers. It is time to act rudely against Iran prohibiting building nuclear arms to support terrorist groups but also time to change the regime for a democracy.

THE IMPEACHMENT PROCESS HIDE YOUR ACHIEVEMENTS

January 23, 2020

Mr. President, you want positive changes for the country and your tool for success is persistence. You signed two important trade deals, one with China, ending partially a two years trade war; the other, the USMCA (United States, Mexico, Canada Agreement) with Mexico and Canada that replace NAFTA (North America Free Trade Agreement). This historic event happened while the Senate developed another important event: the Senate received from the House of Representatives the long-awaited article that declares you guilty of abuse of power and obstruction of justice, and the Senate can begin a trial against you. This latter episode captured more the attention of everybody than the approved trade deal. However, it is important to recognize your effort to complete that negotiation that describes your personality. It is well-known that business is your great passion and there you showed courage and creativity too.

In the agreement with China, it could be easier to give up and end up signing anything than face harassment from everywhere. But you never give up and for two years you faced the attack of farmers, traders, the media, lawmakers, and the whole world. You than China had more to lose with this negotiation because China is a communist empire that doesn't face elections every four years, and you hope to be reelected by those people who are attacking you currently. Also, you have been brave in accusing China of acting dishonestly taking advantage of the US properties for more than 30 years. No previous administrations have accused China openly as you did, saying that China has stolen the US's private property and has not paid fair commercial tariffs for a long time.

Claiming that NAFTA was the worst trade agreement in the entire history of the country also showed your courage. After that announcement, it seemed you were going to have a lot of problems because NAFTA had survived for 25 years, it was a bipartisan agreement signed by former President Bill Clinton, and so far it has been respected. However, there were no protests and business people didn't complain because it was well known NAFTA's agreement wasn't good for Americans. NAFTA caused damages to the country because it was created in a neoliberal epoch when Americans stopped thinking about the country as a whole and instead started to think individually. You wanted to stop American's individuality that's why you brought the nationalist idea of making America great again.

The negative effect of NAFTA was that Mexico and Canada opened their doors for abroad business generously without paying trade tariffs. And thinking to earn more profits, some companies moved to other countries where work salary was low and thus was able to produce cheaper merchandise. They moved to Mexico, China, the Philippines, Vietnam, and more other Asian countries. As a result of that, many Americans who worked in those companies that moved abroad were vacant, growing the social inequality, putting the wealth in few hands, and increasing poverty. You have said many times that you hope that companies will return to the country to produce and generate employment, so America can be great again.

Everything seems to be positive now although people are not sure about anything because the information is confusing, it is an electoral year of elections in the US when everyone attacks each other, everyone lies seeking their benefits and the media is part of the falsehood. Some trade experts have affirmed NAFTA wasn't as bad as Trump has affirmed and also USMCA won't have the expected results. Besides, they said the trade with China neither is going to benefit the US immensely as Trump has affirmed. The time is going to say the truth about this, but at this moment Americans must realize that you have acted with courage.

YOU ARE NOT GUILTY

February 14, 2020

Mr. President, it is known that justice limps but generally ends up catching the criminal in his career, this means that the process was slow but in the end, justice was served. Congress decided today not to impeach you for abuse of power and justice obstruction. Your opponents have affirmed the decision of Congress is disastrous for the country because this allows the president to be above the law and it will allow foreign countries to interfere in the next election. However, your fans have seen the decision with good eyes saying that justice was served, democracy was strengthened and the process allowed you to know that you have been unjustly attacked by those who seek your resignation.

The trial was developed according to the law; the Senate respected the Constitution, the rules, and due process. According to the Constitution, the Senate is the President's natural judge and it can judge him in the last resort. To start the last instance of the trial, the Senate must receive the investigation developed by the House of Representatives through a resolution. This is what the Senate did, following the rules and rejecting the impositions of the House to continue another investigation. The process was developed by hearing first the House's managers, then the president's defense, and finally the vote was taken.

The Senate did something remarkable that was to respect due process and democracy. The Senate followed the rule of justice, considering you innocent until something else would show otherwise. During the hearing, the House's managers couldn't illustrate to the Senate well that you were guilty, that's why Democrats wanted to introduce more witnesses and to continue the investigation there. However, the Senate didn't accept additional witnesses, considered the pieces of evidence were not enough, and exonerated you by voting. In this way, the Senate acquitted you, keeps you in power, and also respected the decision of Americans who elected you as president.

YOUR FRIEND RECEIVED YOUR DEFENSE

February 16, 2020

Mr. President, it became customary to give jurisdiction to the thief and jail for the one who steals bread, said the poet Pablo Neruda; I believe that correcting justice should be an act of justice. A priority in your government has been to protect justice, defend the rights of the convicts and forgive those who have been unjustly accused. The latter has created controversy because some people think you are trying to defend your mates, and thus you are building a banana republic by ignoring the institutions to hide corruption and protecting your friends from going to jail. You have responded by saying that you as president have the power to influence justice to change wrong decisions. And you used the government power to change a jury decision that ordered your friend and longtime collaborator Roger Stone to be sentenced to 10 years in jail.

You affirmed the verdict was exaggerated and needed to be review and changed. The sentence was reviewed in record time and was modified; Roger Stones goes to jail now for no more than three years. That seemed to be an act of partiality because justice had not acted the same in many other cases but in any case, it was an act of justice because there was a mistake committed against a person and you mediated to correct that. In the US, justice and the executive need to complement each other well to correct their mistakes, that's why the constitution gave the president the power of pardon and commute. Pardon and commute are forms used to correct mistakes made at any time by justice or the Executive but in the end, the courts accept the will of the president.

This process that changed the decision from 10 to 3 years has been seen as discriminatory because Roger Stone's forgiveness has been solved faster than others, he is a close associate of you and you spoke mentioning the errors of justice; however, the president's preferences are not only for Stone but everyone without distinction. Some cases can take longer than others but previous presidents have provided mercy to thousands of people, in many cases without observing preferences. For example, President Woodrow Wilson has been the most merciful, pardoning more than 2000 people; President Bill Clinton the last day of his administration pardoned more than 100 people and used this inclination to diminish a sentence against his brother for porting illegal drugs.

You explained the reason for forgiveness because this is being used by enemies to attack the reelection campaign. You said Roger's Stone process was unfair because it developed for two years during Muller's investigation against you and justice found just minors faults. Stone is accused of giving false testimony to justice, obstruction of justice, and altering testimonies. The sum of those crimes cannot be punished with more than one year, the Attorney General William Barr said, adding that 10 years was an exaggerated verdict. Democrats want to take this verdict as a way of discredit you, mentioning that it is not only Stone but many other of your collaborators who have been sentenced previously. They want to emphasize that you are always surrounded by criminals and you have governed with them. Some media has also joined the idea that you have ruled with criminals.

Mr. President, you encouraged to reduce Stone's sentence and could promote forgive other of your collaborators but it doesn't mean you are responsible for what they did or that all your associates are corrupt. There are rotten apples but not all are rotten; you have great officers too who have served the country successfully. Bad and good people are everywhere and all previous administrations have had the same problems; so you cannot be condemned because had some rotten apples. It is always said that we must separate the bad from the good, and that is a good procedure, but those who acted wrongly could change and deserve a second opportunity. I think the President should have the compassion to create a balanced society; he received the power of forgiveness to recognize everyone makes mistakes and deserves a second chance.

YOUR HEALTH IS A CAMPAIGN ISSUE

March 1, 2020

Mr. President, your health is important to do your job; if you must lie about your health to fulfill your mission, it is worthwhile, but health must be above all else. Now that you hope to be reelected it is crucial to take care of your health and because before voting, Americans want to know about the president's health. This matter about your health wasn't clear even before you were elected president. Everything seems to indicate that you were sick before were elected president but this was hidden from people and it was also lied to. It is hard to know your medical record but from the medical history known until now, it is possible to subtract that you have suffered from heart disease and overweight. The clues on this matter are that you expected to visit the Walter Reed National Military Medical Center next year and you finally did this year, also the diet of cauliflower suggested by your doctor.

The truth about your disease started to be a fact after being known that everything started with a lie with the purpose to win the 2016 election. In 2015 your personal doctor, Harold Bornstein, praised your good physical and mental condition, saying that you will be the president with the best health in the whole history of the country. Bronstein affirmed your heart and arteries are perfect and don't have coronaries symptoms. Those words coming from an expert gave confidence to the voters who ended up voting for you. However, in 2018 Bornstein gave an interview and revealed the truth about his words in 2015 before elections affirming that those were not his words but those of the President. He said he copied the words that the president dictated to him and then announced them as his own. This revelation gave evidence that your health wasn't right but the suspicion rose after you suddenly visited the Walter Reed hospital.

The visit to the hospital Walter Reed turns into another lie because you affirmed it was just a routine checkup but some signs show that it was a clinical emergency. It is the case that no one in the hospital knew about your visit and less that you needed a check-up. Everyone knew about this because you arrived there in the afternoon abruptly creating a chaos of security. According to experts, a routine exam was not necessary because the president has one every year and he had had one nine months ago. The President's unexpected visit meant something serious happened. The lie is more evident because a routine analysis can be done by the White House doctor and its medical equipment without the need to go to a hospital. Most likely you suffered a heart attack and had to run to the hospital. You must have a serious coronary problem due to your history of heart disease and overweight that's why your physician has suggested a diet based on cauliflower.

Many would say that the disease wasn't severe because you worked normally the next day however, coronary diseases should always be considered very dangerous. A heart attack can cause death immediately but can also be relieved momentarily followed by careful treatment. Probably the physician relieved you instantly and, thinking about the reelection, you made believe you were fine, you are a strong person with good health. But this isn't like that; the diet based on cauliflower may be indicating that you have cancer, high cholesterol, or some heart arteries have deteriorated. Mr. President, you can deceive people but not the body; it is time to take care of your health by changing bad eating habits, practicing exercise, and relaxing. Four more years as president will demand a lot of work and this can be achieved successfully just by having good health.

JOE BIDEN OR BERNIE SANDERS

March 3, 2020

Mr. President, you can be called a sinner but in the Democratic Party you don't see saints; now it is difficult to elect a Democrat as president, but the best candidate will be a good rival. Finally, there are only two candidates left to compete for the Democratic Party nomination: the former vice president Joe Biden and Senator Bernie Sanders. One of them will be chosen to compete against you for the presidency in November and so it is time you think about who will be elected and how you can face that adversary. Both are good candidates, with long political experience, with different Democratic views, and hard to defeat. Probably you know now who is going to win and also you know how to defeat him because you have already taken some steps to defeat him.

Your opponent to run for the presidency is likely to be the former Vice President Joe Biden. Americans have given Biden their support to compete in the final race with Sanders who started winning the democratic primary elections but Biden emerged after winning in South Caroline and the Super Tuesday. This phenomenon shows Americans respect the democratic tradition and they don't wish to be ruled by a socialist like Bernie Sanders. Americans are voting Biden currently because they don't want a socialist experiment that could bring negative effects. The line leftist and socialism scares people, they don't want to live a bad experience like that of China, Russia, Cuba, Nicaragua, or Venezuela which lacks freedom and for this reason, life is boring without opportunities.

Mr. President, you want Bernie Sanders to be your opponent in the 2020 election because it is easier to defeat his socialist logo than to Biden who is a moderate democrat. However, the former Vice President has many weak points that you know and you will surely use to attack him. A weak point of Biden is that he has always been a bureaucrat who has done nothing significant for the country despite having forty years in politics, including eight years as Vice President which was just as insignificant. Barak Obama chose him as a partner to be his Vice President but he was just Obama's puppet, and Biden took advantage of this high rink to become richer in the company of his family.

Joe Biden's nepotism was found by you when you reported that Biden's son, Hunter, got profitable businesses that were impossible to get if Joe Biden wasn't vice president. Hunter needed really his father's influence because he wasn't qualified to work in an oil company and he also needed commercial references to negotiate with foreign corporations and because Hunter had an addiction to drugs and alcohol. Hunter had the chance to work abroad without experience in an oil company in Ukraine, earning a high salary. It is under investigation why Hunter worked there if that company was investigated for corruption; it is not a good sign the Vice President's son was working in a company accused of crimes. Mr. President, you denounced Biden's nepotism, paying a high price because Democrats started an impeachment process against you accusing you of abuse of power.

The US's future really won't be fruitful if Biden is president because he has shown that he just cares about himself, his family, and his bureaucratic circle but not the country. The country didn't improve considerably during the Obama administration and in the same way, Biden will continue to act. As he has always done, Biden will just give benefits to his bureaucratic community but the poor population will be forgotten again. Additionally, Biden has no energy to develop the country successfully; you nicknamed Biden sleepy Biden because he has no vitality, probably he cannot end even the first four years. Mr. President, you have many facts to attack Biden, it is important to use them effectively to avoid a mistake that the country has to regret.

STARTS THE NIGHTMARE OF THE PANDEMIC

March 19, 2020

Mr. President, the pandemic has arrived and has created an unfortunate crisis. There may or may not be guilty parties about, or it is a moment of bad luck or the same people have sought their own misfortune. You have to think about the causes seriously. You didn't expect that a virus that created a pandemic would damage the good development of the country that you built, it has been a nightmare, but you will know how to handle it. You hoped to compete for the reelection showing a strong economy but it likely will turn into an economic recession probably during the remainder of this year. Also, the media and Democrats blame you for your lack of leadership to handle the crisis which is advancing throughout the country. Until now it is considered that the whole country is infected with Covid: there are more than 6000 people infected and more than 100 dead, Washington is the city with more deaths 55. But Americans need to understand that the progression of the disease isn't the fault of you. I think the fault lies in American culture that focuses on its economy than on its prevention, also the fault lies in its division of power that makes fast decision making and problem-solving difficult, and the cause is that we have all built this sick destiny.

THE PRESIDENT MESSAGES CANNOT BE EDITED BY THE MEDIA

June 9, 2020

Mr. President, I think censorship is harmful to both parties: to censor a president is to deny the tool to govern that is the word, and to deny the word to the people is to stop their social and cultural development. Today you sent a message by Twitter that seeks to rule a protest that has turned violent after a police officer murdered an Afro-American, but the social media platforms handle the message. The message was edited and classified putting a capsule indicating its content is violent and deserves to be reviewed. You considered that social media platforms as Twitter, Facebook and YouTube work with political purpose affecting the good management of the country. The message was edited and this made you look like a tyrant, racist, enemy of the people who wants to oppress the population, while your opponents are shown as good people.

With the message, you wanted to defend democracy. The message could be seen as rude because it didn't use polite words but it was sent to stop the people who were assaulting and firing places. You said by Twitter: "continue violence but bullets will come". Those were not the best words but the message was clear: people have to stop violence or justice represented by police or army forces will act. With the message, you are not motivating violence instead you were trying to govern by making people understand that punishment will come and be hard if they broke the law.

You think it is important to limit social media power because it is proved that media can influence people's minds and the media can use that profit for political ends. Internet social networks are powerful because they currently have not any control over what they do; it is a private system that no one rules. They themselves handle a code of decency called the Decency Act that allows rejecting messages with bad words, violence, and pornography. It is important to reject violence and pornography but messages must be analyzed well before being rejected. Analyzing a message well means looking at who wrote it and the purpose of the message. It was written by the president of the most powerful nation in the world and the message intended to stop violence not to increase it. None of that was analyzed because the purpose was to discredit you by showing you as a friend of violence and an enemy of minorities.

Rejecting bad words in messages is important but Content that is decent and has meaning must be respected. The message is important to the person who wrote it and to the readers who want to know different opinions and knowledge by inferring the meaning of the message. Decent people may feel mad if their messages were rejected or edited but instead, they won't feel mad if their messages are read and commented on. Like you, Mr. President, that felt bad after your Twitter was modified although the message just sought to give security advice. What internet social networks did was the same thing that totalitarian regimes do which is to prohibit free communication. I think you deserve an apology from those networks, saying that you are the president and can govern from anywhere.

RACISM IS NOT AN ISSUE OF TODAY BUT OF ALWAYS

June 13, 2020

Mr. President, if at this time racism is spoken of, it is because the law has always promoted it, becoming a population leveler through the murder of minorities. The issue of racism and discrimination are important topics for reelection at this moment when there are social protests in the country. Those issues gained strength this week after police killed George Floyd, an Afro-American man, putting a knee on his neck until suffocating him. That brutal action of the policeman was recorded and for this reason, people went out to protest in the streets of the whole country. You reacted aggressively because the protesters attacked and robbed businesses, burned vehicles, and attacked the police. You were also not tolerant because you thought that the protest was infiltrated by your opponents and the left. Your strong hand supporting the policy brutality was criticized, but this phenomenon may be the beginning of understanding racism and discrimination in another way.

People expected you to condemn the brutality of the Minneapolis police against George Floyd and condemn racial discrimination. You didn't use words to condemn this but instead used military force to stop the protests. The military measures made you more unpopular, being considered a racist, friend of right-wing extremists, and enemy of black and Latino minorities. Some people have considered that you acted correctly dissolving the protest by using force because protesters cannot apply the law with their own hand. Also, you cannot be accused of being racist or discriminating because that problem goes back many years, these have been a structural problem, and the previous administration didn't do anything to solve it.

Despite racism and discrimination are from many years ago, these have not solved because people have not still learned to respect and being tolerant. Currently, there is more loss of good habits, there are more hatred and desires for power which will make it difficult to solve the problem. Basically, white people hate minorities because they invade their country, have to pay their expenses from their taxes, and they believe the invaders bring just problems and don't do much for the country. Racism does not end either because nothing has been done to eradicate radical groups that hate minorities. In general, racism is not over because the population has not been educated to accept others, minorities have not been taught to give as well, and because the radical groups have remained actives.

From the time of Abraham Lincoln, the 16th US's president, to Barack Obama, the first black president, things have been done to reduce discrimination but it has not been eliminated. In all that time, People have not learned to respect and tolerate others due to the lack of education. Abraham Lincoln's statement was not enough to abolish slavery because discrimination was something cultural; the change demanded education for all. We didn't learn respect at that time and discrimination continued in the form of segregation: whites had their space where blacks had no access. Then Martin Luther King, the civil rights activist, made several marches calling for human equality. In 1964 the civil rights law was established but segregation was not abolished in the US. When Barack Obama, the first black president, was elected everyone believed he would end social discrimination, but that did not happen. Obama reduced black poverty a little but did not make a generous plan to integrate all of society, nor did he put minorities to work, neither did he end extremist right-wing groups.

Mr. President, you cannot solve the racial problem in one day because it comes from a long time ago, it is structural, demands education for all and together we must solve it. You took the first step which was to impose authority by force. Now that there are law and order you could start doing what previous administrations did not do that is seek national unity. National unity is achieved with education for all on how to respect each other and respect human differences. Also providing everyone a job, and everyone contributes taxes, so white people don't feel that minorities steal their taxes. The extremist groups that murder minorities must be finished too; they have always existed, but if they are abolished, culture and society may improve. Mr. President, cultivating national unity leaves behind hatred, racism, and social discrimination; if you may achieve this plan, Americans will be grateful and will put you in the White House for four more years.

THE PANDEMIC CALLS FOR PRUDENCE

June 26, 2020

Mr. President, your goal must be to prevent all social ills, and to achieve this you must take advantage of prudence. Due to the pandemic, you had not been able to make political demonstrations but this week after three months, the first began in the city of Tulsa, Oklahoma. As usual, you wanted to motivate people to vote for your reelection; unfortunately, the rally was a failure because few people participated. People really wanted to participate but they were scared of being contaminated by the virus. This failure served for the media to criticize you, saying that it was irresponsible to plan a rally during the pandemic without applying preventive measures of the pandemic, and ignoring mentioning in the speech the actual social crisis of racism and police brutality. However, you deserve merits because despite the difficulties you did the rally, opened the reelection campaign, and used the discourse to defend the police, the institutions, and the country from violent protesters who want to be above law.

Sadist information like sadist meaning means feeling pleasure by hurting other people, being cruel making him unsuccessful, or destroying him. In Tulsa, the media was sadistic especially television because it was pleased showing repeatedly images of the many empty chairs in the room where you spoke. Also, the camera lenses were opened wide to show the whole room to prove there were just around 6000 people and not 20000 as you expected. These images were accompanied by reporters' interpretations who affirmed that Trump's rally was a catastrophe, and few people follow Trump to open his campaign. This sadistic, destructive behavior has not been applied by the media when Democrats make their rallies, then the media usually affirms partially the rally was successful without showing details.

The speech given in Tulsa was also studied carefully by the media trying to find the worst part to put people against you. The speech worst part was when you didn't mention the police brutality caused against an Afro-American man who was killed by police putting his knee on his neck suffocating him to death. The media repeated that omission, elaborating a bad image of you that describes a supremacist who hates minorities but defends police inhumaneness and white extremists. The other topic the media enjoy displaying later afternoon was six workers of the campaign who were contaminated by the virus, and this was used by the media to emphasize that you were irresponsible in doing the rally during the pandemic putting people at risk.

The media has acted with sadism against you because it never accepted that you had won the presidency; for the media, Hillary Clinton won the presidency. Journalists now want to support the Democrat candidate Joe Biden to win the 2020 election, and journalists are going to play dirty sending all kinds of destructive information. Repeating words and images that say you are a liar, incompetent, corrupt, and racist will be journalists' tactic. Mr. President, you have acted with indifference to the words of the media and don't want revenge, you have just acted to solve the social problems in the best way. You considered law and order by hard hand were the best way because you have realized that socialism and communism have increased and want to destabilize the country. Communists are now afraid of you because you decided to attack them, that's why communists also want to discredit you showing you as incompetent, bad governor, and racists.

However, you need to consider your mistakes because they affect two sensible matters such as the pandemic caused by the coronavirus and police cruel behavior against minorities. About the pandemic, you have omitted to wear a mask to protect the nose and mouth thus sending a wrong message to people who see on you a leader who must follow. Being indifferent to prevention measures is not the best option because that delays the opening of the country and you need this for the economy of the country. Mr. President, you have been also indifferent to racism, discrimination, and brutality of the police by using force to stop protests. Understandably, those social problems come from a long time ago and you are not responsible for it, but being indifferent about it is not the solution because the problem will become worse; so it is time you lead a better society with justice, equality, and peace.

THE COMMUNISM IS DANGEROUS

10 July 2020

Mr. President, I think communism is a good idea on paper but it doesn't work because it enslaves by force, and democracy is a better idea but it doesn't work either because equality is denied by force. Experts in international politics have affirmed China wants you to win the 2020 election because your nationalist policy is very convenient for China to expand communism. According to the experts, you have managed a conflictive, divisive, and not a very friendly foreign policy that may benefit China. China may use your conflicting rhetoric to gain allies, economic, geopolitics, scientific, and social influence in whole the world. However, experts haven't said communism is interested not only in you but in all kinds of presidents to get benefits from them, and thus promote its ideology. No president is an obstacle for the left to achieve its goals; troubled presidents are patiently tried or avoided until a new and better president appears. China would definitely prefer kind and generous presidents who give them everything openly.

Communism is an ideology and political system that want to be imposed on the world by their leaders. Communist ideology, different than capitalism that allows everyone to get properties according to his work efforts, wants everybody to receive equals benefits given by a unique government that controls all the chain production and economic resources. Communist leaders consider communism the fairest system to govern and they seek and use all kinds of means to achieve it. It is not really the fairest system because it restricts freedoms, imposes a kind of people development, not everyone may govern, and everything belongs to the Chinese Communist Party. As the communist purpose is conquering the world, it needs to destabilize the world by spying to steal important information, promoting division, lies, and hatred, and thus weaken countries, create civil wars and take advantage of the confusion. Therefore, for communism, time or the character of presidents is not a problem because they know their goal demand patience and perseverance.

The patience and perseverance of the communists have allowed them really to advance in the world despite having great failures. President Ronald Reagan gave the communists the great defeat initially by attacking them with paramilitary groups everywhere and later in 1989, by using diplomacy to put down the Berlin Wall, the cold war ended in 1991, the Soviet Union was fragmented and Russia became a capitalist country. Despite that failure, communists haven't stopped working to conquer territories and thoughts: Venezuela became a communist country after a military coup; all the communists' countries have formed a block to support each other; Argentina and Mexico have affections for communist countries; China, Russia, and all the communist countries persist in limiting the freedom of their opponents; China continued developing internally fast, while abroad, it has infiltrated many countries with compromising trade relations. And thanks to the former president Barack Obama who opened the US's doors to China generously, the US is now more left party than ten years ago.

Mr. President, Like Regan, communists look at you as a dangerous enemy because you have attacked China rudely from the first day of your rule. You wanted to stop China because it has advanced substantially in the US infiltrating trade, technology, education, and stealing intellectual property. Also, communism has infiltrated the Democratic Party putting the country in danger of turning it into a socialist regime. The OMS has been also infiltrated by communism, so you decided to separate from the OMS and not give it more economic support. The last protests that denounced racism after police killed an Afro-American man suffocating him with his knee was a demonstration that the left has strength in the country because they acted with violence seeking to create chaos and divide the society.

It is absurd that you are attacked for defending the country against communism that has infiltrated all the institutions. China is strong because its philosophy is to practice nationalism; you want to do the same applying nationalism to make America great again, but you are attacked for. Mr. President, you are acting correctly to eliminate communism in the country; however, to achieve this successfully you have to stop the social inequality that is 75 percent of poor people while the rich are 5 percent and have all the wealth of the country. Communists are actually taking advantage of the US's social inequality to create chaos and nonconformity. I think that reducing social inequality can end communism in the country and capitalism could flourish again. If you are reelected have to practice social equality but if you aren't, your successor will know that this is vital.

YOU CAN SAVE THE WORLD FROM COMMUNISM

20 July 2020

Mr. President, Communism, and democracy are born from repression and slavery; communism followed those same steps, democracy evolved demanding equality but at this time democracy resembles communism. You know China has a plan that is going to achieve before 2050 about being the most powerful country around the world, to discredit democracy, capitalism and spread communism to many more countries. People are used to seeing the US as number one; but could China achieve its plan of becoming number one, and will it be beneficial to the world or as destructive as it needs someone to save it? China has progressed considerably that he could be thinking now that has enough power to get what he wants. China wants to defend its territory and wants also to get territories that China considers yours such as Tibet, Taiwan, and Hong Kong. China plans to get strong internally and externally defending its symbols, economy, making its security strong, restricting freedom, and putting pressure on other countries economically to get benefits and thus expanding communism.

China's 2050 plan is more about communism and it can be terrifying for the world's freedom and justice. If China's plan sounds terrific, Americans will have to find one of their superheroes to save them or someone who hating communism like you. The first thing to say about China is that this country hates democracy and capitalism; China's way of government is different than a democracy that means lack of freedom, lack of individual opportunities, and lack of individual development. China's form of government is through a unique and permanent party (the Communist Party) and a unique governor. China's president governs quietly because there are no political elections as in democracy, making political development more stable but unfair to the development of human life. The government manages all the natural resources, the production chain, there isn't private property and everything belongs to the communist party. People cannot protest; ideas and thoughts against communism are banned; the use of social networks is restricted, and religious beliefs different than Buddhism are excluded.

Some democratic countries practice too the restriction that communism makes but they hide it hypocritically by exalting the word democracy; however, freedom can be more available in democratic countries than in communists. Ultimately Chinese President, Xi Jinping, has given some drastic steps to restrict freedoms, teaching that he wants to fulfill the communist plan before 2050. Xi Jinping has created a spying program to denounce anyone who is against China and its government. This program was designed to give benefits to those who denounce and punish people who attack communism. In general, the President doesn't want that anyone to form ideas about country divisions or western ideas, that's why Xi wants to know his people's thoughts.

An example of what is the loss of freedom in China is in the Muslim community of Uighurs that its members are considered terrorists by China Communist Party (CCP) because Uighurs want to form their own territory in China. The Uighurs' idea is considered offensive because it tries to steal national territory. To avoid the Uighurs' project, the CCP has created detention centers where they are educated towards socialist ideas. Uighurs who are found congregated in mosques, talking about division or against China, and disobeying Chinese laws, are placed in those centers where they must work hard, learn the Chinese language and communism. Outside where the Uighurs live, the CCP controls Uighurs' private life, their mosques were closed, and they just receive information and news from China.

The same model applied to Uighurs is the one that the Chinese government uses to control society. This model means controlling the private and commercial life of everyone especially foreign people and companies. This idea goes further to secure its current borders and recover the old ones, and this started by issuing a security law to restrict freedoms in Hong Kong. This intrusion into the democratic life of Hong Kong means that Xi Jinping wants the full recovery of this country and has anticipated achieving his 2050 plan. China couldn't interfere with Hong Kong's own system until the end of 2040 but he did enacting a security law that allows the arrest of people who are against Chinese policy. That same security policy is used against foreign companies that promote democracy, ideologies different from communism, speak against China, and disrespects its symbols.

Mr. President, Americans need to reflect on whether communism can solve the problems that democracy has not been able to solve such as poverty, social inequality, violence, racism, social discrimination, and environmental destruction. Communism may solve those global problems but the price is to change the free life system; democracy too could improve people's lives if it works equal and honest policies without affecting freedom. Mr. President, you believe as well as China that nationalism is a powerful way to improve a nation, and through nationalism, you have been governing. With this form of governing, probably you are anticipating the 2050 plan of China and you don't want the country to be left behind allowing China to be more powerful. You understand democratic nationalism is different than communist nationalism, both help to improve a nation but democratic nationalism preserves freedom while communism denies it.

YOU HAVE TO ADMIT MISTAKES

25 July 2020

Mr. President, you are doing what Mr. Amine Ayad's quote says about recognize mistakes: "be humble to see your mistakes, courageous to admit them, and wise enough to correct them". It is no matter how big is the mistake or the time it took to recognize the mistake, it is very important to admit and correct them. The pandemic caused by the Covid 19 has several responsible especially China who seems created the virus. Nevertheless, the media has accused you of being responsible because you have not led the problem well, that's why contamination grew to be the US with the highest number of deaths. Your policy has been to give confidence to people so that they are not afraid of anything even death. You have appeared in public without a mask, have not demanded distance, and have suggested home medicines to attack the virus. Until now, your police has not worked apparently because you follow your instincts and not the recommendation of your scientific advisers.

Mr. President, as the problem has been growing, it is time to realize mistakes and change policies, following the advice of experts but without forgetting your instincts. So far it is not clear if you have admitted mistakes as the last rally in Tulsa in June when you put people's health at risk, but now it is clear you want to correct those. You probably changed your mind because you were warned of the mistake that could affect the reelection but also you understood the disease won't stop if radical prevention measures aren't applied. So far after seven months of the pandemic, more than four million are contaminated and one hundred and forty thousand dead. These figures have made you understand the seriousness of the problem and this week you started to correct mistakes by canceling the convention in Jacksonville, Florida, to promote your reelection affirming that it is more important to protect the country and the health of the people.

You now are asking people to wear masks, keep social distance and wash their hands frequently, even sometimes you wear a mask, something you haven't done before. Besides you started to lead White House press conferences frequently to provide data on the pandemic, inform about government actions to eradicate the disease, and insist on applying preventive health measures. This is the kind of leadership people like to feel and if this is sincere and effective they will appreciate it very much. However, many people have doubts about the sincerity of your actions because you haven't yet recognized the scientific authority, you want students to go back to college although that sound contradictory to stop the virus, and people also think you changed your mind because it favors your reelection.

Mr. President, it took you a long time to recognize mistakes and correct them because you wanted people to understand the need to live a better and normal life. For example, you disagreed with scientists and the OMS because those are bureaucrats who just want money but haven't worked with passion for the country preventing disasters. You said scientists and any kind of organization must show positive results for the development of the country instead of thinking about being rich, gain fame, and being in bureaucratic meetings. I think you believe people can feel healthy if they can work and have skills to improve their lives instead of being lock up in the house. You want children may go back to school because the future of humanity is cultivated there, and also you believe they are not at risk of getting sick because they are young. Of course, it took a long time to understand it because the plan of making America great again demands taking dangerous risks as you did, but everyone could take risks too to help develop the country.

THE PRESIDENTIAL ELECTION WILL BE A RELENTLESS BATTLE

28 July 2020

Mr. President, I believe that the biggest rival now is not Joe Biden but the goal you want to achieve. If you win reelection, you will learn from your efforts, not from your rival. But if you focus on the rival, negative emotions such as discourtesy and lies will be applied. The media has highlighted insistently many negative factors about your way of governing, hoping those remain in people's minds to vote against you affecting the reelection. Specialized surveys have demonstrated that if the election were today you would lose by a high margin of 10 percent, even you would still lose in states where Republicans have always won. This is a serious problem because there is not much time to maneuver, just three months left to convince people that you are better than Joe Biden. It seems hard to reduce the ten percent margin and you will have to find another option to continue ruling. The other option was mention by the former candidate Hillary Clinton and it is that you would not recognize the election results trying to stay in power.

Vice president Biden's ten percent margin in his favor could increase because the media multiply by four the errors made in your government. For example, this week that your national security adviser, Robert O'Brien's covid test registered positive for covid, the media has remarked about the large number of your collaborators who have been contaminated with covid. The media insists on that and adds comments about the numerous contaminants and deaths in the country. Your enemies want to hold you responsible by saying that you have mishandled the health crisis being a danger to the country and the world. So that negative image about you is circulating everywhere affecting your credibility and people's voting options.

Reversing that bad image in just one hundred days before the election will be very difficult. To reverse that problem you must continue being yourself without changing your entrepreneur character. Americans have seen that you are a brave man who works hard and likes to solve problems yourself directly without fear. You have applied a strong hand so that violence does not grow in the country, also you have ventilated the problems of corruption and bureaucracy existing in the previous administration and the Democratic Party. But what most people like about you is that you ended the governors' hypocritical way of ruling and the media of communicating.

Many Americans think you haven't acted wrongly leading the pandemic because you have wanted to build trust in people by saying not to worry about death, after all, every day people die from different causes but life must go on. You said people die in car accidents daily and for this reason, it is not forbidden to drive or sell cars nor is the country closed. People die of malaria every day in the world and the OMS hasn't declared that is a pandemic. Many people like your idea considering the pandemic a hypocritical lie, but many others disagree saying that the seatbelt has saved the life of drivers, the malaria vaccine has also saved many people and also the mask has saved many more from covid 19. The points of view are divided and thus divided people will vote in November.

On Election Day the distance between you and Biden can be reduced although Democrats have thought about everything to win. They plan to win both the popular vote and the Electoral College vote, by avoiding the mistake made in the 2016 elections when Hillary Clinton won the popular vote but lost the Electoral College vote and thus lost the presidency too. So the war will be focused on getting the battleground states' college vote where is the largest population and their numbers will determine the winner of the presidency. Democrats lost the 2016 election due to college vote because indirectly is the way the US chooses its president, so they are going to do anything to get that majority. Because the election could be fraudulent, you must be vigilant in watching and listening to what happening that day. If you see something suspicious on Election Day, you must declare the election as fraudulent and request a recount of votes, and if it is worst, you can call for new elections. I think the Democrats' desire of winning the 2020 election is not because you are a bad president or have ruled badly, it is because traditional politicians cannot see someone like you teaching them with character and without hypocrisy.

NEGOTIATE LIKE RONALD REAGAN

8 August 2020

Mr. President, late president Ronald Reagan and you used similar ways to negotiate that you need to apply now to face the actual social crisis that involves several problems. Democrats want to put you between the sword and the wall to force you to negotiate a big budget that can show Democrats as saviors of the current crisis and you as responsible for everything. The financial aid basically goes to support the unemployed caused by the pandemic and depending on the amount, Americans will feel thankful and thus will vote in the next election. Mr. President, if you lose this negotiation Democrats not only hold you responsible for unemployment but also for the current economic crisis, deaths caused by the covid-19, racism, police brutality, lack of authority, and leadership.

Putting you against the wall to force you to negotiate serves the democrats, if they win the negotiation, to discredit you and thus win the election. Democrats did the same in 1990 against the late President George Walker Bush to make him lose the election. In his campaign, Bush promised not to raise taxes but he finally did to support the troops that sought to remove Saddam Hussein from Kuwait. Democrats didn't care about the 500 000 soldiers were fighting in Kuwait, they just care to show that Bush has broken the promise not to raise taxes. Americans charged Bush with a lack of character and did not re-elect him in 1992. Democrats want to do the same to you but I think it will be difficult because you have proven that Ronal Regan's negotiation technic has worked very well.

The dilemma is between accepting what the House of Representatives wants and accepting to be attacked by the House. Democrats can attack you on many fronts that are sensitive matters for the population. One of them is the pandemic caused by the covid-19 that has infected more than 4 million people and has killed more than 150 000. Democrats perfectly can say you are a murderer because you didn't handle this problem well, didn't set an example allowing people to disobey the prevention regulations. Because of this lack of leadership, Democrats also can affirm you destroyed the economy, jobs, health, and education. Racism is another sensitive problem that is hot currently after police killed an afro American man suffocating him with the leg on the black man's neck. Many people around the country and in other countries protested against the brutality of the police, but you didn't accept the protest and attacked the protesters with the use of police force. So Democrats can accuse you of defending police brutality, and being against minorities and democracy.

Mr. President, you have faced many pressures in the past and you have solved them well thanks to following your instinct and also following the teaching that President Ronald Regan left behind. Regan taught to say no and to look for other solutions. You have applied Regan's rule well. For example, when you were looking for funds to finance the border wall with Mexico, Democrats didn't want to give you any penny for it, but you didn't accept the denial and looked for alternatives. Then you applied the longest government shutdown in the US history of 34 days and you got finally more than one million dollars. But since that was not enough money, you declared a national emergency to get money from other sources, until you got it. To face the present crisis you probably won't accept pressures and look for better alternatives. I think you should think about another way to get funds and use them not only to relieve unemployment as Democrats want but to alleviate all social sectors. This form of negation and solution, surely Ronald Regan would have applied.

YOUR BROTHER ROBERT DIED; HE LOVED YOU BUT OTHERS DID NOT

17 August 2020

Mr. President, as children we all want to have a brother, you had four who gave their essence to you that is how you learned to laugh passionately among many other things. Today Saturday 15 sadly your youngest brother Robert died and I want to give you my condolences. I think this moment is a hard one for you because Robert was your closer brother and as you mentioned he was your friend. Usually, when someone dies, people different from family use that moment to learn more about the family of the deceased. This behavior increases if the family belongs to an important social group as it happens with you and all your family. Mr. President, because of this, today through news the whole world knew more about your family and the family relationship that it is the same as other families with similarities and differences.

You were five siblings including you: two women, Maryanne and Elizabeth. Three men: Robert, Fred, and you; you were in the middle of them. Now there are only three siblings left after Fred and now Robert died. The relationship with Robert wasn't always good but you appreciated Robert's loyalty that's why you considered Robert a good friend. The relationship with your older brother Fred, who died forty years ago, was conflictive due to Fred's different views that you and your father did not share. You made fun of Fred because he wanted to be a pilot instead of working in the family businesses. In the end, Fred did what he wanted and became a pilot, but Fred did not overcome the addiction to alcohol and died young.

Differences between people are resolved depending on how each one reacts. For example, your brother Robert after having dislikes with you tried to be more friendly and faithful. Robert didn't want to be a businessman like you but he wished you were successful. Fred's daughter blamed you for his father's failed life. Mary's revenge became real recently after she wrote and published a book about some of your bad habits as a person and Trump's family problems. Mary published the book quickly because she has felt angry with you for a long time and wanted it may affect your reelection. Robert tried to persuade Mary not to publish the book by affirming that his brother Donald is a good person and the Trump family is respectable. Mary never changed her mind and published the book before her uncle died.

Mr. President, from those incidents you learned from both Robert and Fred that's why currently you, more than anyone, love, respect family, and human values. You learned a lot from Fred and continue learning from him because as Fred was an alcoholic, you understood alcohol takes people's life, so you decided never to consume it. At this moment that Fred's daughter published the book, you probably are reflecting about your brother Fred and may wish to be now with him and to have been a better brother. Probably you acted badly but you did not do it with bad intention, you just were looking to defend the family business. Please don't feel regret, just try to be a better person at all times. From Robert, you learned loyalty and brotherly love. Brotherly love is very strong in you, although loyalty is not so strong because you are cautious and distrustful as all businessmen are. However, Mr. President, I think it is better to be loyal to yourself to your values and principles as you are; that's what makes you a real leader.

THE 2016 ELECTION IS DIFFERENT FROM THE 2020 ELECTION

22 August 2020

Mr. President, Americans must understand that whoever offers a lot is because they are not going to deliver. This is the case with Democrats who have not kept their promises while you are short on promises but many actions, it is because they think about the elections and you about the future of the country. Two months ago the media insisted that Joe Biden was leading in the polls by almost ten points; the remark had the intention of weakening your image, create discontent making you more unpopular in the future. Mismanagement of the pandemic has been the main reason for discontent because the virus does not stop and continues to contaminate and kill people. The pandemic has also affected the economy and thousands of jobs have been lost. Besides, racism has reawakened in the country again after people realize there is police brutality against minorities such as African American people who are murdered in unjust conditions by police. The polls gave ten points in favor of Biden, however this last week the percentage has been equalized and both are in the game. Why?

That poll phenomenon happened the same in the 2016 campaign when two months before the presidential election Hillary Clinton was up in the polls but you end up winning the presidency. The race is uniform now and it is important to know what things made you go up in the surveys to continue working in the same way. The 2016 election was different than this one; then people were looking for something else from the candidates. Americans felt very disappointed because they expected from Barack Obama and Hillary Clinton more achievements but Obama's administration was just eight years of high bureaucracy. In 2016, you picked up the votes of those hopeless people and won the presidency.

In this election other things can motivate people to vote, for example, they would like to see your goal of making America great again become real. As you started to build this dream, Americans would like to see concluded it. People understand that is better to continue the programs than stop them; for that continuity, Americans will vote for you. So far you have done many things to achieve the American dream. In the case of the pandemic, people shouldn't understand it as a failure but rather an opportunity to understand that life cannot be stopped and people need to keep fighting. You said the arrival of the virus is not a failure, it is another disease like the flu that must be attacked but unfortunately will cause deaths. You have transmitted that confidence to people so that they do not feel fear of death and continue to work normally. As a leader, you have taken the risk without wearing a mask and accepting physical distance, and that's what Americans like.

THE PANDEMIC WAS A PLOT

November 3, 2020

Whenever there is a gathering of wolves it is because there will be sheep's food; this is what the Democrats and the media have done trying to hunt you down. I am watching the news now from a CNN television channel and a reporter is interviewing a person in a Florida bar that was used to cast votes for this election. The reporter and the interviewee both wear masks but the many people at the back of the bar dancing and talking neither wear masks to protect themselves from the virus. This seems to be hypocrisy of CNN because this channel is criticizing the president every day for not wearing or demanding the use of a mask. CNN doesn't care people wear a mask but they do care that the president; and now that the president and his wife Melania has caught the virus, the criticisms are more intense. All this malicious and fake news from the media, the surprising way in which the virus emerge, and the rapid way in which the president is relieved may suggest that the pandemic was an invention to overthrow the president.

If all those themes are connected we will have the following story: the virus Covid 19 was created in China, however, this country has recovered rapidly while the world is infected and closed its borders affecting the world economy. President Trump has affirmed that this phenomenon has occurred because China, the left, and the OMS work together to destroy the US but especially to overthrow him. This may have a lot of truth because the president has opponents everywhere who do not want his reelection and to achieve this, the strength of the president which is the economy, should be attacked. The failure of the president was achieved by deteriorating the country's economy and with the help of the media, making people believe that there was a pandemic.

The plot goes like this: first, the country's economy was affected because the world's borders were closed and second, this was not a pandemic as the OMS let it believe. To determine what a pandemic means, people must look at the 1918 Spanish flu that in less than a year killed more than 40 million people. The current pandemic has been an anguishing created by the media that needs news to justify its existence. This virus in less than a year has killed a little more than a million people in the world, but if it is looked at closely, this figure is very much lower than the number of people killed by malaria or flu, or car accidents each year in the world. And for this reason of deaths, the OMS did not previously declare a pandemic calling for the closure of the world, or traffic authorities haven't forbidden to drive vehicles.

Mr. President, from the beginning you understood that the pandemic was a plot to end you, so you continued to work on your ideas and ignore the pandemic. Of course, you had to close the country as the rest of the world did, affecting employment and the economy totally, but you sought to create trust in people by showing that there was no need to be afraid. You very seldom put on the mask, nor did you demand people wear a mask or keep distance to prevent infection. Your idea was that people live a normal life living with the virus as they live now with other diseases. It was true that some people were going to die but the same happened with other diseases that killed people daily. The media did not understand your ideas and attacked you daily, recalling the number of deaths and contamination from covid 19, but they never showed how many people died from other diseases daily. The media attacks were brutal and sought to discredit you to weaken you in the polls.

If people want to discover that the pandemic was a false invention just look at your fast and positive evolution after being infected with covid 19. Mr. President, on October 1 you gave positive for covid 19 and five days later you were recovered, working normally and even you looked younger and slimmer. According to all those scientists that you reject, a person suffering from covid 19 should be isolated for several weeks and that an older adult hardly survive, but it should be much more difficult for you to survive having a life as frenetic as yours. None of that happened and you recovered quickly, demonstrating that the covid 19 is like any other current disease that kills people but also has relief. With this you wanted to create trust in the people, confirming that there was no need to close the countries and their economies but rather people had to live with the disease as it is done with other diseases. Face with the closure of the world and its economies nothing could be done because it was proposed by the OMS that is a world health organization that everyone obeys. Despite this, the virus has not evolved as a pandemic killing more than 50 million people as it did in 1918 because it was not a pandemic it was a plot to avoid your reelection.

ILLEGITIMATE IMAGE OF JOE BIDEN

November 24, 2020

Mr. President, the government can become a nightmare for Joe Biden because it is tied to a fierce bureaucracy and the idea of illegitimacy. The election is lost but there is a possibility to create the illegitimacy image of the Joe Biden winner. There are three areas where Biden's illegitimacy can focus, one is the characteristic of the election two, that the Democrats never recognized your victory in 2016, making your government difficult, and three, Joe Biden's son, Hunter, committed crimes during his father government as vice president; it remains to be seen if Hunter received his father's support. Regarding the characteristics of the election, this changed the way of voting due to the restrictions caused by the Covid 19 pandemic. Voters voted in masse by mail for fear of getting sick. With this system, which you had predicted would be cause for fraud, Joe Biden won the presidential election. Mr. President, the illegitimacy of the election that you can argue is that, due to the particular nature of the election, it was necessary to provide other revision controls for each vote throughout the country. It is very possible that many of those votes had false signatures, or that the voters were people killed by covid. You could not verify every vote because the political system is federal and each state has its own rules. For this reason of being an election that got out of control and that demanded more controls is that it can declare illegitimacy.

The second part you can argue with is that the Democratic Party never accepted that you won the presidency in 2016 and sought to remove you from the government by accusing you of crimes that they could not prove. You really could not rule because of the selfishness of the Democrats and you should ask to be repaired by ruling for another four years. The third part deals with Hunter Biden's crime of doing business with corrupt foreign companies from Ukraine and China. This episode could be serious if you can prove that Joe Biden helped his son by using his power as vice president of the United States. This investigation must be done independently of the government because it is the way to confirm the participation of the vice president and his illegitimacy.

THE DOUBLE STANDARDS OF THE MEDIA

December 20, 2020

Mr. President, in the media there are no positive changes because they appear honest and responsible but they are the opposite, mediocre and false. Thank this false media you can see now the difference between what was the beginning of your government and this of the new president Joe Biden. The current environment is one of boredom, hopelessness, double standards of the media, of continuing the lie of traditional politics and covering up the corruption of the political bureaucracy. In 2016, before the presidential elections, the fierce media attack against you is recalled, saying that you were unable to govern because you had no experience, that your intelligence was poor and that there would be local and global setbacks due to your lying and conflictive character. Everything about you as your family, your friends, and your past was investigated and criticized without compassion, meanwhile, the Democrats sought to cover up the corruption committed by Secretary of State Hillary Clinton who put the country in danger using the mail system irresponsibly.

When you take over the White House, the Democrats already had the plot to remove you from power. They had spied on your campaign for the presidency and by one unsubstantiated indication or another claimed that you had won the 2016 elections with the help of Russia. Russia's interference in the elections was considered a crime that determined the theft of the elections from the candidate Hilary Clinton. An investigation was ordered which, for two years, failed to find serious evidence to formally accuse you. In those two years of investigation, the media attacked you unfairly and rudely daily, giving you little space and energy to rule. But now that Joe Biden is assuming the presidency, there is a serious investigation with evidence showing that Hunter, Joe Biden's son, did business and worked with corrupt foreign companies, the media seeks to ignore that investigation by shutting up the microphones. The double standard of the media is evident and disconcerting, which confirms what you, Mr. President, always proclaimed and that is that the media is a system of false news, manipulators that are destroying the country and the world.

POLITICAL DEATH

January 14, 2021

Democrats have tried to remove you from power during your four years in office but have not succeeded despite facing a lengthy investigation and impeachment. Now with less than ten days to go before you deliver the presidency, the Democrats seem to finally cause your political death. The House of Representatives has authorized a second political trial against you for motivating an insurrection in the Senate to stop the certification of Joe Biden as president. I believe that this time you have gone too far creating certain arguments that can cause the dismissal as president or political death to aspire to any public office including being president in 2024. The best thing would have been to accept defeat and have delivered the presidency without scandals, this way you would have the doors open to competing for the presidency again. Now this will be difficult because even if the Senate acquits you, there will always be a precedent that you caused an insurrection and that is not forgiven by American law.

President, you knew that you played with fire and continued to take dangerous risks because taking risks and always winning is your nature. Joe Biden's group of friends is powerful and produced Biden's victory; because otherwise, Biden would not have won considering that in forty years as a politician he did nothing for the country. That group was of course your enemy and among them were Wall Street, Silicon Valley, the retired military bureaucracy, and the political bureaucracy cultivated by Barack Obama and Hilary Clinton. All of them joined forces and financial resources to create a fraudulent vote that was going to be difficult to prove fraud due to the country's federal system in which each state is independent and determines the way of counting and inspection. Who would believe and even Biden was surprised to receive a little more than 80 million votes because he himself knew that he did not deserve that. President, the nearly 75 million votes filled your winning ego, it clouded the thought of you refusing to accept defeat. The insurrection was your last resort to reverse Biden's triumph because the courts and the Supreme Court denied your request to review the count of the elections. The insurrection went wrong and you are forever marked as a conspirator.

What you could do now to at least save your future peace of mind is to resign before being removed as Richard Nixon did, hand over power to Vice President Mike Pence, and Pence grant you pardon. The pardon would prevent the ordinary justice from persecuting you, however, you would be politically killed for fomenting the insurrection that tried to ignore Biden as president. The other thing you should do is take things easy because what was done is already done and you cannot go back in time. The tranquility that you need now could be given by understanding that history must record you as the president who turned the country and the world upside down, contradicting the political order and hypocritical traditional ways of governing. The 75 million Americans who voted for you realized that they have always been misled by traditional politicians who promised equality and justice but never delivered by dividing power and wealth among a small group of corrupt bureaucrats. This same teaching of the political hoax has to serve people around the world because injustice and inequality are widespread.

This episode of insurrection leaves two unfortunate lessons that describe how traditional politics annuls people's social rights. One lesson is that there is no justice in the country and the other is that the opponent is annulled by taking away his dignity. Before the insurrection, you looked for all legal means to prove that there was fraud in the elections, and all of them were denied. And now, after the insurrection, you are sensed and all communication channels are closed to you in the style of any communist country where there are no avenues of defense. This injustice and sensitivity prove that the country is run by a powerful group of wealthy bureaucrats who manipulate the elections and install the presidents. Also, this proves that the country has been governed for the benefit of them, the bureaucrats that are why social inequality, racism, police brutality, illegality, crime, corruption, and drug trafficking never ended. All this disastrous social panorama is allowed to advance to have at election time every four years an issue that justifies the campaign and the permanence in the government of the same corrupt ones forever.

In this negligent way, political diplomacy works and solves the problems, letting things go by and doing things so that the problem continues and remains the subject of a political campaign every four years. President, you omitted diplomacy, you were rude and a liar, but these were defense mechanisms to solve never-ending problems. Omitting diplomacy and being rude, you opened the eyes of millions of Americans to show the deception of traditional politics that has more than 100 million people living in squalor while they enrich themselves enormously. This lesson should serve Americans to propose a new way of governing. It is known that the country belongs to the rich and the poor, but dignity must be given to all. Discrimination ends up omitting the distances that exist between the public official, the policeman, and the military with the public. People must be served by public officials diligently, with respect, and government policy must be equitable distribution, cooperation, and provide entertainment rather than conflict.

CONCLUSION

Making art is very difficult because it demands to reflect on the soul of art which is the reflection of reality. I learned about that phenomenon by observing a movie when an American man, while he was visiting Paris, asked a famous French artist to make a painting of him. The painter was well known as a smoker, drinker, and likes women very much but as well as great sculptor and painter. The American man asked the painter to do the painting quickly because he needed to come back to his country in a week. The man expected to receive the painting after one week but the artist always postponed work, spending his time with women, drinking, and smoking. However, the reason for delaying the work was not vices but rather that the artist did not see anything special in the eyes of the American. After the two men spoke and got to know each other for almost a month, the artist discovered in the American's eyes a spark of sincere emotion that allowed him to finish the painting.

In a figurative situation that a famous artist wanted to pain politicians, this would be impossible because they do not reflect the truth. The artist could say something different about painting President Donald Trump because he is not a politician and can display his character easily. I am not saying that it is not possible to paint a traditional politician, I' am saying that won't be art because it does not tell the truth. It means it is impossible to draw a traditional politician correctly due to his lack of honesty and responsibility. Politicians have always stated by words their compromise to apply freedom, justice, and equality but until now those words have all been a lie. The lie of the politicians has hidden their personal essence that's why it is impossible to make art in them.

This imperfect character of traditional politicians is one of the conclusions that is discovered during the government of Donald Trump, but the bold and determined character of Trump who has never been a politician but knows the social shortages caused by the permanent deficiency of the system is also discovered. Art describes the genuine and spontaneous reaction of everything; Trump has a particular genuine character, that's why the artist finds it easy to draw him. Donald Trump is a narcissist, self-center, liar, treacherous, tireless worker, dreamer, spontaneous, and radical conservative, and all that character is easily reflected in Trump's expression. Nothing can be hidden in Trump's big round face. His big eyes, wide smile, thick eyebrows, and good figure demonstrate personal security, dominance, and perfection. All Trump's emotions, passions, and intentions cannot be hidden because they arise and are marked on his appearance. Artist could easily reflect in his painting Donald Trump's ambition and evil together because they appear spontaneously on his face as a whole.

Trump's actions and reactions are not separated from his facial expression because everything is a set that forms his nature. Trump can be serious with a confident look with a firm voice saying something that may be a lie or the truth such as Nancy Pelosi is treacherous or he wants Mexico to pay the border wall. He may also be smiling while telling a lie and it sounds convincing because he believes it and because his nature is always to attract attention. So everything he says, be it lie or truth expresses it with force and security because his being believes it that way and because he wants to convince the public. The same goes for actions, Trump has to be doing or saying something because it is what gives him recognition, and wants to be seen as a winner who has done spectacular works like his casinos, clubs, hotels, and the Trump Tower. Trump is not stopped by ethics or laws when it comes to meeting a goal. As president, he knew what the country and the world needed, that is why worked tirelessly bypassing the system to get everything.

Nothing scares Trump, everything that happens he enjoys. His enormous security is given by his desire for success and recognition. In his four years as president, Trump faces attacks from all quarters and he chanted the truth to everyone until the last day. To the media, Trump rubbed out the truth that it was a fake system of news. He called the Democrats lying bureaucrats who want to overthrow him to stay in power. Trump faced a two-year investigation and responded strongly to the media and democrats every day until he was acquitted. He openly told the communists' countries thieves of the United States and the freedom of people. To the multilateral pact of the environment and the health organization like the OMS, Trump also called them bureaucrats and traitors. No president had thought as much of his country as Trump did, rejecting globalization, group of countries such as the G-7, G-20, the European Union, and communism. He was not afraid when the pandemic hit and he continued to believe in the country's economy over the disease. Trump faced the accusation of abuse of power as normal for asking a foreign country to investigate his opponent Joe Biden. Trump enjoyed this impeachment process and used it as publicity for the reelection campaign.

Trump made news of all kinds every day using any form and medium. He used all available means of communication especially twitter from where he accused, insulted, and lied without diplomatic or ethical consideration. For this behavior, Trump was attacked by all the media but in reality, Trump's constant messages were those that gave life to the media, the country, and the world. Around the world, Trump was talked about because he turned political diplomacy on its head singing the truth to any person or organization that opposed his nationalist ideas. Trump also generated all kinds of actions, some more spectacular than others, but it was evident that they sought to attract attention. For example, moving the North America embassy from Telavi to Jerusalem, creating controversial international comments; meet with the North Korea dictator on the border of that country; assassinate the most prominent general of the Iranian army, Soleimani, using drones; propose the purchase of the island of Greenland; greatly transform the celebration of the country's independence day; and most surprisingly, go against all the rules to prevent the pandemic.

All these actions as well as his messages on Twitter, in many cases, Trump developed them with lies and bypassing some legislative laws because it was the only way to advance quickly in his government goals and to defend himself from attacks by the media and his opponents' democrats. In this way, he managed to overcome the many difficulties and begin the government works. Americans did not care if Trump lied or ignored the laws because the polls never fell despite being investigated and then accused, they were excited to see that the president sang the truth to all the traditional politics of the country and the world and that also there were achievements that had never been seen. The faith to have a voice that denounces the traditional bureaucracy, that raises its voice against the untouchable world organizations, that there are effective development actions, and that the political tedium of always ends had ended with Trump.

Trump was accused by all of being a liar, but there has been no worse lie than the diplomatic lie used by longtime politicians in complicity with the media to cover up his poor performance. It can be remembered when the previous presidents ended their governments the feeling that they did nothing, that everything continues in the same social inequality and poor development is generalized; however, they are applauded as heroes and will always be special guests from the media. They are rewarded for doing nothing and they continue to be rewarded, turning politic into a hoax that has become a habit. Diplomacy is not only used to improve relations between nations but is used in all areas of life because it means kindness, courtesy, and good manners to handle a difficult situation. The problem with diplomacy is that silence, doing nothing, procrastinating, became the solution to all problems. This method of doing nothing disguised with good manners that are used in politics is the one that has the country and the world in Deja vu of the same levels of social inequality and underdevelopment. The lie of diplomacy compared to the open lies of Trump is truly deadly because that is only concerned with preserving the bureaucracy. Trump did not use diplomacy at all, but he showed results in all social areas and made politics a little less hypocritical.

Nothing in his irregular way of governing affected Trump because the result of the 2020 elections was known and more than 74 million Americans voted for him. This is a vote that the Republican Party has never gotten. However, that number of votes was not enough to win and with the defeat, Trump shows that he does not like to lose and that he does not give up easily. President Trump did not recognize Biden's triumph, stating that there was a fraud and that he is going to demand the election for the Supreme Court to decide. Election experts have said Trump's lawsuit will not go through because an investigation is costly, time-consuming and so far there are no signs of fraud. Probably Trump will cede the presidency to Biden but he won't accept Biden's triumph and file a lawsuit before the Court affirming that he is not the one who does not accept Biden's triumph but it was the Democrats who did not accept his triumph in 2016 and from the first day to the last the Democrats attacked him, preventing him from governing his four years.

In this regrettable way and already missing the daily political turmoil ended the presidency of Donald Trump; however, I think that he left important teachings to improve politics, the country, the world, and the faith and dignity of the people. Trump turned politics around by finishing diplomacy to discover the lie of politics, which is to always maintain levels of social inequality. The election showed the enormous division that the country has: Biden with the political bureaucracy and Trump with those tired of life without progress. The voting system based on gathering the 270 votes of the Electoral College is the main cause of division in the country because some states have more influence than others in the victory. This division of power as well as the confrontation between parties is what has the anesthetized society denying it a voice to achieve its rights. Because of the political division, the race war has never ended, and Trump defended himself against racial attacks by imposing law and order because traditional politics, not him, are responsible for racial discrimination.

From now on, the majority of presidents will probably adopt Trump's way of governing when the legislature denies the executive's projects. Democrats and the media said that Trump was unaware of the system, and that was true, but he did so within the norms that the law grants the president to issue executive orders to solve immediate problems. Joe Biden has already said that he will issue executive orders from the first day of his presidency to erase what Trump did; in this case, the media is not criticizing Biden as they rudely did Trump. The lesson of this is that presidents will now use their power with dictator overtones. Besides, the role of the media will have to improve because Trump has been the only president with the courage to say that the media broadcast false news. Trump affirmed that during the four years of his government, Americans finally opened their eyes to see that the media does not show reality but what they want, that the journalist is more important than information, the media do not educate but generate violence and their work is so mediocre that they never get a survey right.

The most important part of Trump's legacy is the nationalist line that he always promoted and applied. "Make America Great Again" was his anthem that was sung the way regimes do without being heard outside. As part of the anthem, he fought for the construction of a huge wall that would cross the border with Mexico to stop crime and illegal immigration. His idea was to strengthen the immigration law to accept foreigners with merits to live and work in the country. For Trump, it was very important to secure the country for the Americans, but also to regain global respect by showing economic power. The economy was his most important goal because Trump refused to comply with the restrictions of the pandemic that was infecting and killing people and preferred to encourage the normal life of the economy. Trump was widely criticized for not leading the pandemic well, affecting his political image, however, he took the risk and managed to revive the economy during the third quarter of the pandemic.

As his idea was for the country to be the first for the Americans, he handled it as if it were a regime that rejects multilateral groups, globalization, and any organism that divides lowers the role and economic resources. For this Trump broke diplomacy and openly asked the European Union countries to pay fair tariffs, and China created a trade war to show the commercial abuse of this country to the United States for more than thirty years. He also refused the Paris environmental pact because he considered it costly and not very credible, and also broke ties with the OMS because he considered it joined China to promote the pandemic and affects its government. For Trump, globalization was not harmful but the procedure harmed the country and benefited China. The United States was not receiving fair trade rates and all kinds of crimes were flooding the country for having soft immigration laws. China instead flooded the world with low-priced products, paid low trade fees and communist was a closed system, with regime laws limiting freedoms to control crime and protests. What globalization was doing was guaranteeing rapid progress to China in all areas, and Trump was not going to allow it.

Trump really became for many hope and the way to regain dignity. For generations, others like kings, emperors, politicians, commanders, and preachers have built people's hope without positive results. Ordinary people placed their hope on them and waited for them can provide a better life for everyone. However, wars and domestic violence never ended; poverty, economic and social inequality have increased; racism, gender, and sex discrimination have also created hate and violence. In the US, for example, Americans believed that everything would change by naming the first president of color, Barack Obama. But it wasn't like that; Obama was from the same bureaucracy that wants to keep the status quo of social inequality. That's why in the last few years, feeling hopeless, people have opted to build their sense of hope by protesting and not selecting those traditional leaders.

Americans were tired of seeing the endless social progress directed by traditional governors and decided in the 2016 election to name Donald Trump as president, a rich person without political experience. Democrats say Trump lost by more than three million votes the popular vote; however, most of the 50 million people who voted for Trump were people without a social voice, people who had nothing to lose and no hope. Now Donald Trump became a model who first teaches to build strong his house to provide security, order, employment, and social security for everyone. His nationalist thought and his courage to face and solve promptly country's problems, it has made us believe that hope is in our hands and everyone and every country has the responsibility of building his future.

The 2020 presidential election with more than 74 million votes in favor of Trump has shown that the country is divided between a dissatisfied population and another well-off that has always ruled the country unfairly. With the arrival of Trump to the presidency, this social time bomb armed by traditional politics with indifference towards social and economic equality was discovered. With Trump, it is discovered that there is no political work for the people but the ambition of power to maintain a bureaucracy. With Trump, the dirty and rude game of politics is recognized, but also the hypocrite that has always deceived people by promising justice but they never ended racism. With Trump, it is recognized what the policy should be, which is to work tirelessly to people and for the people. With Trump, people discovered that there is hope to appoint a courageous leader who will defend them and cultivate the dignity of all. And with Trump, the Republican Party made great progress, having control of the Senate, with more seats in the House of Representatives and more control in the states and at the local level.

Biden won the presidency, and his job will be to end social inequality to defuse the current social bomb. But if Biden cultivates the same bureaucracy, Americans will have Trump back in four years to feast on his messages, lies, and strong tone of hope. Personally, I believe that Trump will return to the presidency in 2024 because he has millions of followers and because Joe Biden is appointing the same group of bureaucrats that worked with the former President Barack Obama, which means that negligence and irresponsibility in government will continue, with the same levels of inequality and social injustice. And because many Americans are already disappointed with Joe Biden because he tries to cover up the crimes committed by his son Hunter who did business with corrupt companies in Ukraine, China, and Russia and has omitted to pay taxes. But what worries them most is this close connection of Biden with the communist countries because he opened the doors for them to abuse the generosity of the United States.

Finally, with everything that happened during Trump's four years, it is discovered that another way of governing with a more democratic force must be adopted. There is much social and cultural disorder that globalization has left, therefore the micro government is the only solution. Micro-government means governing by observing the smallest details that occur in every society. For example, migration rules should be more precise, detailed, and fair. There should not be a criminal war to persecute the illegal immigrant, but rather clear rules that allow them to live with dignity. Human behavior must be precisely regulated in areas such as personal hygiene, hygiene in all institutions and businesses. Louis Pasteur, the French biologist inventor of the pasteurization system, stated that there are viruses and bacteria everywhere, and asked the population especially doctors to wash their hands vigorously; these words spoken more than 100 years ago must be taken seriously and governed on that basis. Caring for the environment must also adopt a form of micro government. The management of natural resources such as water, air, and the earth with its resources must be governed with precision to make them renewable. This micro-government must focus mainly on educating the population so that they have the knowledge and understand why and how the natural environment is protected.

Building the dignity of the population is the most important, it demands millimeter work because dignity has been destroyed and this is the basis of order, peace, and social development. Building social dignity requires ending the existing social distances between the population, public officials, and the military. Racism, discrimination, disorder, and social hatred have not disappeared because social repression continues. Democracy can have its social and economic differences but it should not have human contempt or discourtesy. Governing to the millimeter to build appreciation and respect between the different social sectors creates the most important thing in society, which is its dignity.

If Trump returns or Biden wants to succeed, they must create the dignity and hope of the people. This is not easy because the United States belongs to everyone and belongs to nobody because it is a country of immigrants. Nor is it easy because presidents do not manage to govern for the people but themselves, enlarging their circle of power. The distance between the people and public officials is enormous and this is evident because in most countries these officials do not mind taking people's calls and attending to their social needs. However, there is a way to create dignity and it is precisely by ending the social distance, preferences, and bureaucracy that distances the population from public officials. It is well known that self-esteem increases when a person is listened to, observed, and cared for with care. This physical and emotional attention between people is what makes them human with self-esteem. Americans will feel respected if the public official is on the same level as the people by providing courteous and effective attention. The social distance that has existed so far is what does not end racism and police brutality.

This is a society of rich and poor but dignity must be provided to all people. All Americans should have health care, quality education, a monthly salary, housing, security, and prompt attention to their needs as a community. Indeed, Trump did not meet those needs either, but he opened people's eyes to fight for their dignity. Cultivating respect for all should be the job of the next presidents and is achieved by reducing the distance between the authorities and the population: The people must be treated promptly and respectfully by the police, the military, and the public official. Ending that bureaucratic distance that separates the population from the public official will provide dignity and respect for all. Speaking of shortening the distance between humans and all politicians, Trump more than anyone knows that it is through the cell phone using technology that people may ask for help and cooperation promptly without bureaucracy. Just as Trump could be heard by the world through his tweets, people must be promptly attended by any public official using the cell phone. The moment the bureaucracy of the distance between the population and the public official is over a society that respects itself cooperates and cultivates its dignity will be created.

Epilogue

It is only a few hours until Donald Trump hands over the presidency to Joe Biden, but the drama of Trump and his influence on American politics will continue for years or, I would say, forever. The drama for Trump will continue as soon as Joe Biden is inaugurated as president when the second impeachment trial is brought forward, this time for motivating an insurrection in the Senate to prevent Biden from being certified as a winner by Vice President Mike Pence. This episode generates anxiety among the powerful enemies of Trump and expectations among his followers, which are more than 75 million. Trump's enemies are confident of achieving his political death so that Trump cannot aspire to any public office including the presidency in 2024. This political death is very likely to occur because insurrection is a serious crime that without exceptions is forgiven. The Senate will likely acquit Trump because it is a Republican majority, but Trump will not be able to save himself from continuing in political life because justice does not forgive the insurrection. It is also likely that before the end of the presidency, Vice President Mike Pence will grant Trump a pardon to avoid future harassment by the ordinary justice system, however, the antecedent of the insurrection will always be in force and will deny Trump the possibility of continuing in politics.

On the side of his followers, they hope to continue listening to the voice of Trump who denounces the fraud and illegality of the presidential elections; for him to prove the crimes of Hunter Biden and to continue his nationalist policy of making America great again. It will be difficult for them to accept that their political leader has been politically annulled. They may not accept it and decide to continue the acts of insurrection, which, as some policy experts' claim, could lead to civil war throughout the country. Whether an internal war occurs will depend on how Joe Biden handles this issue, and the best thing would be to seek dialogue, end the political persecution of Trump that has not stopped since 2016, and motivate democracy with the participation of the opposition included that of Donald Trump. The whole world will be witnessing this unprecedented political drama in which a president during his government is formally accused on two occasions and the process of the second accusation will take place as a former president. In this unprecedented process it will be known if the Democrats won by removing Trump from political life or if the Republicans managed to defend their leader by keeping him politically alive and preserving his harvest.